A GRADUATE OF THE UNIVERSITY OF LIFE

A GRADUATE OF THE UNIVERSITY OF LIFE

By
Frank Burns

REWORD PUBLISHERS

2004

Published by
REWORD PUBLISHERS
3 Syddal Crescent
Bramhall
Cheshire SK7 1HS
www.reword.co.uk

© Frank Burns 2004

ISBN 0 9536743 8 X

Printed and bound by
GOPSONS PAPERS LTD
INDIA

This book is dedicated

To my parents, who kept their honesty and integrity in the face of great poverty and hardship, and who set a fine example. And to my wife and children and our seven grandchildren who never asked for anything I couldn't give them.

ABOUT THE AUTHOR

Frank Burns (Christened Francis) was born and raised in Blackburn during the Great Depression of the thirties. After the sketchiest of formal education, during which he arguably set records for absence and attended four different schools, he left school at fourteen with neither qualifications nor skills. In four years he had no fewer than seven different jobs, and at eighteen was called up for National Service in the RAF, where his natural command of English Grammar and accurate spelling landed him on a clerical course. The typing skills he learned on this are now being put to good use. Returning to civilian life, he renewed his wanderings, working as cinema projectionist, dye-house labourer, iron dresser in a foundry and machine operator in a rubber-works before finally settling into the paper industry. In 1953, he married the girl whom he met while both were working in the cinema and now have two sons, two daughters, and seven grandchildren. On Boxing Day 2003, they celebrated their Golden Wedding.

Made redundant in 1992, he turned to drawing cartoons, using a natural talent and no formal training, and had his work accepted by magazines such as 'The Author' and 'Punch.' After having an anecdote published in the prestigious 'Reader's Digest,' he decided to try his hand at writing, and in collaboration with his younger son Christopher (also a self-taught artist) he has published a history of Blackburn Rovers. He is currently working on his second detective novel.

A GRADUATE OF
THE UNIVERSITY OF LIFE

'Let not ambition mock their useful toil,

Their homely joys, and destiny obscure;

Nor grandeur hear, with a disdainful smile

The short and simple annals of the poor'

Thomas Gray.

INTRODUCTION

And Destiny Obscure

I am a graduate of the University of Life. There was no diploma, no mortarboard and gown, but it provided the best education that poverty could obtain. Four years after I left elementary school, and into which I had crammed a measure of experience in no less than seven different jobs, I received the 'King's Shilling'. In this instance, so far advanced from the days of the press-gang, which gave the item its title, it was a postal order to the value of four shillings, or a day's pay in the armed forces. Once accepted – as if there was any choice – I had morally agreed to serve King and Country for as long as the Government of the day deemed fit. Too young to drink alcohol, too young to vote or to have the key of the door, all privileges reserved for the attainment of majority at twenty one years of age, off I went, not to seek my fortune, but to follow in the footsteps of my father and older brother, who between them had clocked up eight and a half years of military service, not counting my father's six years in the pre-war Territorial Army.

The conscription net had trawled wide and deep, and only the minnows had slipped through its mesh; ergo, as I was now inducted into the Royal Air Force, I was not a minnow, but one of the various species safely gathered in for a period of National Service. I had reported, as instructed by my call-up notice, to RAF

Padgate, Cheshire, on the twenty first day of March nineteen forty nine, the first official day of spring, in the face of a biting easterly wind that was carrying rods of sleet that stung and chilled.

This was my first time away from home, and I had not made an auspicious beginning. Hands deep in raincoat pockets, head bowed against the sleet, I had walked past a groundsheeted sentry and through the gates, between the dilapidated Spitfire on the right hand and the Hurricane on the left, each tired symbol of the Battle of Britain standing forlornly on its tiny patch of sodden turf and looking as dejected as the sentry. A few yards further on, I was startled by a hoarse bellow of pure rage.

'Get those hands out of those pockets you horrible, detestable, loathsome .....'

I shuddered. Some poor lad was getting a rollicking for trying to keep his hands from freezing in this bitter weather. What a way to address people, even if they were in the RAF. I looked around for the subject of this tirade, which, I now saw issued from the mouth of a huge RAF policeman who stood in the doorway of the Guard Room, a ramrod figure in blue battledress with white-topped cap and white webbing belt and gaiters. Of the victim, there was no sign, although the voice ranted on.

' ..... *cretinous civilian* ....'

The penny – very belatedly – dropped. I was the sole civilian. Or rather, as the policeman now informed me, *ex*-civilian. I was now, apparently from the moment I passed through the gates, in the Royal Air Force, and I was to swing my arms to shoulder-height, straighten my horrible, wretched, round-shouldered, misshapen form and smarten myself up or something awful and immediate would befall me. I felt that his warning had arrived a little late. I removed my hands and began to swing my arms as though my life depended on it, and as I neared a hangar I saw that in its shelter huddled a company of groundsheeted figures, who welcomed me with a chorus of 'You'll be sorrrrrrrreeeee.' And here again, I felt the prognosis was belated. I had been sorry since I entered this miserable place of dripping groundsheets, wooden huts, puddled roads and general air of utter dejection.

At the top of the road was a signpost bearing a crudely-painted hand in black on the white board, the forefinger pointing stiffly onwards, and underneath were the words 'New Arrivals Hut 212.' I kept on, now mercifully out of sight (or at least vocal range) of the policeman and after a while arrived at Hut 212.

Entering, I found myself facing several rows of young men sitting on wooden forms, with their backs to me, and being addressed by a corporal from a dais at the far end of the room. Upon my entry, the voice of the corporal fell silent and he gazed over the heads of his captive audience and glared at me with smouldering eyes, and in the silence, a hundred or so heads swivelled to look at this interruption. Rather like one of those Western films when a gunman enters a rowdy saloon and there is immediate silence. I felt naked under their scrutiny, and not without reason; every one of those young men had, at his feet, a small suitcase. I had none. With my usual carelessness, I had merely glanced through the call-up papers, and under the impression I would be kitted out immediately upon my arrival, as per those wartime American films, when people like Bob Hope were issued uniform before they had quite got their civvies off, I had simply put on my raincoat as though going to work and caught the train. This inattention to detail on the call-up papers condemned me to three days without a proper wash, using my hankie to wipe my face over each morning, acutely conscious of the sideways glances of my new comrades at morning ablutions. Fortunately, I shaved only about once a week, and so went unshaven and undetected until finally kitted out. I tried not to wilt under the scrutiny of these well-informed young men, whose cases obviously contained the requisite soap, towel, toothbrush and shaving kit, but the corporal could not neglect such an opportunity.

'And where the hell have *you* come from?' he demanded.

'Blackburn,' I said. I noted that many of those strange faces had taken on a sort of cruel expectation. I had seen the same expression in newspaper photographs of Nazi thugs baiting Jews, and I tried to stand straighter.

The corporal took a breath like a diver about to go deep, and slowly he raised his hand and jabbed a finger at the two stripes on his arm.

'What do you think these are?' he screamed, 'Toffee bars? You address me as Corporal at all times.'

There were sniggers among the faces.

'Now then, lad. *Where* did you say you came from?'

'Blackburn, Corporal.'

His eyebrows shot up towards the peak of his service cap. 'All that way? By yourself? And have you bloody well *walked* it?'

There came a chorus of sycophantic laughter, and I felt a slow blush climbing my cheeks. The farthest I had ever been before was to Blackpool, for a half-day with my maternal grandmother when I was five years old. To someone of my limited travelling experience, Cheshire might just as well have been China, and as I had not been completely keen on joining up anyway. I had taken advantage of the guidelines in the papers that ordered me to report 'between the hours of 0900 and 1600,' and as it was now about 1510. I believed I had been rather generous with my remaining civilian time. The corporal obviously didn't agree, but something in my bedraggled form must have fanned a tiny flame of humanity, for he suddenly sighed and told me to go over to the counter in the corner and get a cup of tea. Now a word about that cup of tea. Perhaps it was that I was cold, miserable and thirsty, or perhaps it was because I seized on that *beau geste*, but that cup of tea was without doubt the best I ever had in the RAF. Which, on reflection, may not be the highest accolade.

For the rest of the day, we were marched from hut to hut, we signed documents, read documents, and studied documents.

We trudged to a dreary cookhouse for tea, a meal of instant mashed potato, one sausage of dubious content and a spoonful of baked beans in thin tomato sauce, augmented by two slices of stale bread and a tiny knob of margarine and a mugful (they *had* issued us with a mug and 'irons' – knife, fork, spoon) of some sort of tea which, if left for a few minutes, settled and separated, the solids like sand, on the bottom, and clear water on the top. I had heard some half-jokes that bromide was added to the tea, as a precaution against us running amok and violating every female who crossed our path, but that RAF camp, with its dripping billets, sodden turf and streaming groundsheets rendered such a drastic step superfluous, for, tea over, we trudged to our assigned billets. I had never been so miserable and downcast in my up to then short life. Later, as I lay on the rough blankets that covered the three 'biscuits' on the wire-framed bed, listening to the mix of dialects from this company of strangers who were to be my comrades, I felt tears of homesickness pricking my eyelids and was glad when lights-out came at ten o'clock. Or rather, now that I was no longer a civilian, at 2200 hours.

CHAPTER ONE

Very early Days

My arrival into this world coincided neatly with the start of the Great Depression, my first cries sounding on Armistice Day 1930. I like to imagine that my birth occurred exactly at the stroke of eleven, when, from the heights of Corporation Park, one of the old cannon captured in the Crimean War was fired, its dull thud reverberating over the town and everything coming to a halt for the two minutes of absolute silence observed in memory of the hundreds of thousands of young men and women who perished in the Great War. Of course, this is sheer licence on my part, but as I never knew the exact time of my birth, it never did any harm to invent a little romance. God knows there was precious little of it in our lives.

My parents married, with no money and no home, but with much urgency, in June 1927, and my father simply moved into my mother's home, the humble two-up, two-down rented by my maternal grandparents at number ten Pink Street, off the stretch of shops, pubs, church and cinema known as Bank Top. And there my elder brother John (but always called Jack, like my dad) was born on the twenty seventh of December. Hence the urgency; there were many short-term pregnancies in those days.

Number ten had flag floors, a fireplace in the front (living) room and one in the front bedroom, a tiny yard with a lavatory at the end and a slopstone in the rear downstairs room which served as both kitchen and washhouse. In this little house lived grandad Bamford, grandma, mother, father, Jack and finally me. By later standards it was little better than a hovel, but in those days, it was something of a better-class home, for it had its own yard with lavatory, while many streets had houses that shared these on a communal basis. The lighting was gas but only in the living-room and front bedroom, and this was fed from a meter into which pennies were fed as necessary, always subject to availability.

When I was about one year old, my parents got the key of number eighteen, and we moved in, the little house identical to our former home, except that it cost a shilling a week more in rent, because some time before, the landlord had made some 'improvements.' What these were, my parents never discovered, but anyway, here they set up home, with the bits and pieces of furniture donated by kindly neighbours who had little enough for themselves, but who always somehow managed to help out those less fortunate then they. Of which there were many.

As my infant memory matured, two faces, blurred at first, began to firm up and become the ever-constants in my life. One was male and had rather unruly dark hair and grey eyes, the other was female, gentle, with long dark hair, brown eyes and a mouth that made comforting noises and hummed soothing lullabies. My parents; John William Burns and his wife Winifred, nee Bamford.

As I grew, learning to walk and talk, the guiding light of my life was Jack, whom I followed with the devotion of a puppy. Dad lost his job some time about nineteen thirty two, and from that time until the outbreak of World War Two, he was on the dole. This was, of course, of no importance whatsoever to Jack and me, and we loved our parents dearly, as they loved us. Life for our parents was hard, but it never ground them down, and there was always something they could find to laugh at, even with empty pockets and often empty bellies.

One of my earliest memories is that of a scorching day in June nineteen thirty-four, when I toddled in from play and went to investigate the strange sounds coming from the front bedroom. Climbing the uncarpeted stairs on hands and knees, I had reached about two thirds of the way up when a terrifying figure in starched white appeared at the top, and regarding me sternly, this phantom ordered me 'downstairs, at once, young man.' Now the actual words meant nothing to me, with my strictly limited vocabulary, but the spirit in which they were rendered left no room for doubt. Down I went, to be picked up by dad and taken to grandma's, where I was made to remain until later in the day, when dad came and took me home to greet my new sister, Joan, a tiny beauty with raven black hair and hazel eyes.

And so, on the thirtieth of June 1934, our family became complete. That very night, over in Germany, the Nazis celebrated the infamous 'Night Of The Long Knives,' an event that would have a profound effect on my father. And of a few million others, as the world knows

CHAPTER TWO

First steps

Countless millions of words have been written about those days of the Great Depression, and no doubt they were the hardest of times for ordinary people, but for children, they were halcyon days, when it always seemed to be summer, with long, hot days spent playing happily, often in bare feet, on the scrubbed pavement. Safe among friends, relations and neighbours, our activities monitored by the policemen who patrolled frequently and kept a benign eye on the toddlers and a judicious one on the older ones, who were more inclined to mischief, which was often dealt with by a swish of a cape on the backside. Policemen were minions of the law in those days, not clerks.

Talking of policemen, I was still barely toddling when I was brought to their attention and can clearly remember being questioned by this being in dark blue and helmet, who seemed to rise as high as the rooftops. But if I felt fear, I cannot recall it, merely a feeling of awe and wonder at such majesty. The reason for my interrogation was an injury to my next-door playmate, Billy Duxbury. He and I had been playing quite happily in our back yard, climbing onto the top of the tiny covered area where stood the dustbin, and leaping onto an old bed-spring that was awaiting collection by the council men. The springs acted like a sort of trampoline, especially when jumped on from this height of about five feet, but the wild glee as we bounced was curtailed when Billy did a sort of involuntary somersault and landed awkwardly. Result, one broken forearm and one visit by the man in blue, who, if not striking the fear of God into me, certainly ignited a profound respect for the law he represented. With hindsight, that clearest of all faculties, he was merely making sure that the injury to Billy had resulted from the fall and not from any other source. How many poor children would benefit today from such political incorrectness?

Numbers seventeen, nineteen and twenty one, the three houses that reached to the junction with West Street, were demolished, and the space cleared ready for the building of the new 'Bank Top Workingmen's' Club.' Living directly opposite, we could watch the men going about their work from our own doorway, or the edge of the kerb, and on wet days, from the comfort (?) of our living room. There were no earth-movers in those days – not the mechanical sort, at any rate. The work was done by gangs of men in shirt-sleeves and corduroy trousers wielding pick-axe and shovel, and who often sang at their work. Here I found my first hero to worship. Hector drove the lorry that brought the sand, cement, beams and all the other things that went into the building of the club, and carried away the rubble. Sometimes he took me along for a ride and I can still recall the thrill of standing in the cab, gazing in wonder at the road rushing under the wheels, and now and then I would turn to study Hector, whose hands and feet were never still as he manoeuvred his lorry between trams, bikes, cars, lorries, buses and scuttling pedestrians. To me he was a magician, and I never lost my fondness for lorries.

Jack was fascinated by the men carrying hods full of bricks or mortar, and climbing the tall ladders to the brickies working on the upper floor. One morning, the foreman, 'Mad Jack,' called him over and presented him with a miniature hod he had made himself. Jack was over the moon with this, and strutted about as though he was one of the gang, with a few pieces of brick in his hod. Mad Jack, chewing tobacco and with his thumbs hooked into his braces, watched his new man with an amused eye, and called him over. Adding another couple of pieces of brick to Jack's hod he instructed him to take his load to the man on the high scaffolding. Jack turned a nervous glance in the direction of number eighteen, where my mother stood watching, then went over to the ladder and placed a foot on the bottom rung. Craning his neck, he looked up to where the brickie waited, a wide smile on his weather-beaten face. Another step, now Jack had both feet clear of the ground, and his glance our way was one of near terror, barely controlled. Mad Jack chewed steadily, his eyes fairly dancing with amusement as Jack attempted the third rung, but this proved too much and he descended with shaky legs and moist eyes. Mad Jack sighed, spat tobacco juice, and, producing a penny from his waistcoat pocket, paid him off on the spot, all the while giving sly winks to my mother. The penny took the edge off Jack's embarrassment at being sacked so arbitrarily, but from then on he kept a distance between himself and the builders.

The club, when finished, was a noble building of dark red rustic brick with stone facings, sparkling in its new livery of green and cream, and with a brand new sign over the door, illuminated from within after dark, that told the world that the club was part of the CIU. To us kids, it was a shining beacon, and when we were a little older, and we got the opportunity, we used to gather in the doorway on wet evenings, to talk about football or cricket. One of the members used to come down every Friday evening with his little Jack Russell terrier, have a couple of pints, then collect his sweep tickets. He used to select one of us to wait, holding the lead, and when he left – which might be as much as an hour later – he would give the lad a penny. We jostled and sometimes fought for this perk, even though an hour on a wet and cold night was a long time. I suppose the man was really doing us a kindness, for he could as easily have tied the lead to the drainpipe by the door, but it was certainly a penny well earned.

In those hard days, there was a large army of itinerants, including rag-men, street musicians and singers and tramps, otherwise known as gentlemen of the road, and often we would be treated to a song from a ragged 'Cavan O'Connor' sort of young man with a pleasant bar-room tenor and perhaps accompanied by a partner on either cornet or accordion. I remember one such entertainer who strolled down Pink Street, accompanying himself on the banjo, and gave a plaintive rendering of 'Mammy Mine', the hit of the moment:

'If I had a million dollars,
It would not be worth a dime,
Not without that love of yours
O Mammy Mine....'
'Ev'ry time I write a letter,
There is love in ev'ry line,
But not like that love of yours
O Mammy Mine....'

The man was young, good-looking in a rough sort of way, and wore trousers that were frayed around the bottoms, a mop of unruly curls, and a jacket that hung on his lean frame. The soft Irish lilt in his voice brought the women to their doors with moist eyes and ready purses, for a great percentage of the inhabitants were of Irish stock, including my own grandparents, and they, who had so little themselves, could never let such a deserving case go by without a copper they could ill afford. And if the high notes faltered a little shortly after the pubs opened, or the lines ran into each other, well, what wandering minstrel could sing properly with a dry throat? It was a long time later that I recalled this scene, and thought that the man who penned the heart-wrenching lines probably lived in some California villa with a swimming pool in which to cool off when the labours of writing such drivel left him limp and sweaty. But at the time, none of those good, naïve, and honest folk entertained such cynical thoughts.

One-man bands, knife sharpeners, street entertainers, they somehow all scraped a living from those poor streets, and even provided, on occasion, little gems of amusement for the kids. Foremost among these was the old man who toured the area with his rickety old cart, pulled by a bony sad-eyed *Rosinante*, and on which was fastened a miniature merry-go-round. With half a dozen wild-eyed tin horses dangling from worn barley-sugar poles, their flanks almost bereft of the once-bright dapples and the patent leather reins replaced with frayed string or cord.

It was difficult to tell which creaked loudest, the cart, the horse or the man, as they bumped and jangled over the paving setts. But their arrival was a moment of great excitement to us, for on the cart, whose faded paint suggested it had once been blue, was a sack filled with bright red rubber balls, coated in French chalk and bearing the fishy smell of new rubber. Now a ball of any sort was a thing to treasure, and these were brand new, never before touched by childish hands or feet, and something to be coveted when yearned for and treasured when won.

On first spotting him, we would run into the house and beg for some old rags – of which our house, at least, seemed to have an on-going supply – and with arms laden to the Plimsoll Line, we would queue impatiently for our offerings to be judged. If you had enough, he would reach into the sack, and with the air of a genie fulfilling a wish, would produce one of the balls. The lucky recipient, heart thudding, would grasp it and run off, followed by a bunch of hangers-on who had no rags of their own except those they were currently wearing. Soon the street would echo to thuds, whoops, yells and angry shouts from neighbours whose windows were under threat, whilst the less fortunate would climb aboard for the consolation prize, clinging to the sticky pole while the old man, once the full complement was mounted, would begin to crank the huge wheel that powered the merry-go-round.

Slowly, at first, the horses would begin to move, gaining speed as the old man's sinewy arms spun the wheel faster and faster and soon we would be hanging on for dear life, our cries of glee rapidly rising to screams as we went faster and faster, below a churning sea of upturned faces, above, the spinning rooftops. With the centrifugal force threatening to loosen the more feeble grips, the old man's eyes blazed with a fierce glee. And when we were beginning to think that the ride would end in our being flung onto the paving setts, smashed like so many china dolls, there would be the first faint signs of a slowing of the speed and gradually our hearts would slow with the horses, until at last, the horses stopped. We would slither gratefully down, reeling drunkenly to the safety of the heaving pavement, and sit with our backs against the wall and try not to look at the lurching houses opposite until our stomachs had stopped churning and some colour had returned to our faces. Never again, we would vow, when the world had stopped spinning sufficiently for us to join the game of football. But by the time the devil's contraption came again, all the discomfort and terror would have died completely, and there we would be, hoping for a ball, but quite content to ride the horse. You could always tell when the old man had been round; some kids were playing football while the rest were sitting quietly, with faces pale green in colour, and with their backs propped against the walls of the houses.

One day, my mother made the bargain of a lifetime, paying a couple of pennies to old 'Boss' Leek, a rag-man of good standing in the neighbourhood, for a home-made pedal-car. I can recall the excitement as he reached it down from its place of honour atop the laden cart, with its cargo of old clothes, empty jam-jars and donkey stones, and deposited it onto the pavement. Of course Jack had first claim, being the older, and he would pedal furiously up and down the pavement, while I patiently waited for a turn.

But there was one less patient than I who coveted that home-made bone-shaker. He was the neighbourhood Charley Peace in miniature. Bobby lived lower down the street, a bandy-legged kid a little older than me who, like Peace, once he saw something he wanted, had to have it, then and there, and regardless of consequences. If the car was left unattended for any length of time – say eight or nine seconds – there would be a sudden flurry of activity, a rattling of wheels and off would go the car, with Bobby bent over the wheel, bandy legs pumping, and Jack chasing. Not only did he 'take and drive away,' he also resorted to outright theft, for if he spotted the car in our back yard, he would nip over the wall, as agile as a monkey, unbar the gate and manhandle the car up the steps, all in complete silence. On one such foray, Jack spotted him making off with it, and demanded that he bring it back. The response was a large piece of broken drainpipe, flung with deadly aim, that badly cut Jack's face and nearly cost him an eye. His dad used to belt him and we always felt sorry, but nothing stopped him for long.

I was always a little afraid of Bobby, for he was a real hellcat and loved to fight, but one day something he did, (for the life of me I can't remember what), pushed all fear and caution out of the frame, and we went at it hammer and tongs, rolling on the pavement in front of the club. I was so mad I didn't care how much he hit me; I just wanted to knock hell out of him, and when we were eventually separated by one of the club members, I was surprised to find that I had had the better of the exchange, and from that moment on, he treated me with wary respect.

Before I was born, poor Jack caught double pneumonia, and for a while, it looked as though he wouldn't survive. But Dr Malik saved him, and although Jack was little more than skin and bone, he recovered, but from then on, my mother was terrified of him falling ill and tended to wrap him in cotton wool when the weather was nippy.

My mother was pregnant with me when, one brisk day, she dressed Jack in his hat and coat, covered his head with a bob-hat, and sent him to play on the 'flags,' as the pavement was called, under the aegis of grandad Bamford, then retired, who was sitting on a chair on the pavement watching the world go by. Worn out with manual labour at seventy – the retiring age at that time – and with a pension of ten bob a week, that was about his sole pleasure. It was washday, when the clothes were boiled in the copper boiler in the kitchen/wash-house and scrubbed on the solid table, a mandatory feature of every house.

'Keep your eye on him, dad,' she instructed, but her admonition was dismissed with a wave of the walking stick on which he rested hands and chin in his ponderings.

'Och, ye make too much fuss,' he said, 'the child's all right. Get about your business.'

And so she did, only to be startled a few minutes later by an angry shout from the street. Dropping the posser, she ran outside and found the driver of an LMS railway horse steadying the beast with one hand and holding Jack by the collar of his coat with the other, whilst demanding of the street in general whose was this lad?

When my mother claimed him, the pale-faced driver handed him over, under the inquisitive gaze of grandad Bamford, four doors up, who was wondering what the commotion was about.

'Just be thankful it's this horse, and not my usual one,' said the driver, who went on to explain that while he (the driver) had been delivering a parcel to the club, Jack had walked under the horse's belly, the bob on his hat tickling the great Clydesdale and causing him to move slightly and snort in both surprise and annoyance. Jack, sublimely unaware of the proximity of disaster, walked out on the other side of this equine arch. Had it been the driver's usual horse, the result would have been too horrific to even think about. This information no doubt did my mother a power of good, especially in her 'delicate' state, and she made sure Jack was not left out of her sight to amuse himself.

As I said earlier, Jack was my guiding light as I grew, and I followed him everywhere and tried to emulate his every act. But just when I was in most need of his companionship, he started school, and although this meant that I received more attention from my parents, I longed for the promised day when I too would be so far along life's road that I could attend school too, which goal was about the limit of my aspirations.

The bottom end of Pink Street was occupied by half a dozen little businesses; Harry Heath's foundry, James Coates's joinery business, a narrow stable yard belonging to a coal merchant, William Harrison, and Clayton's garage on the odd side. Then George Dewhurst's builder's yard, Eric Ainsworth's textile machinery parts and Joe Cox's general metal dealer's on the even side. The bottom end was completely blocked off by the wall of the weaving-shed of Bank Top mill, and there was an oversize wicket painted in bilious yellow paint where we played cricket on warm days, using the length of the narrow pavement fronting Dewhurst's yard as our pitch.

We made our own rules where circumstances demanded. The wall of Dewhurst's yard cramped the leg-side, so all shots that rebounded from the wall had to be caught one-handed, to make it fairer. Disputed 'out' decisions were settled by the challenge, when the bat was reversed and the handle used to defend the wicket, the ball being delivered underhand along the ground, from the middle of the wicket. The colloquialism for this was 'The Pegleg.' If the ball went over into one of the yards, it was a case of 'six and out, or none and in,' when the batsman had the choice of six runs added to his score, or re-starting – subject to the ball being retrieved – with no score. All good, common-sense solutions to problems that could have caused friction in less tolerant circles.

CHAPTER THREE

Schooldays

St Anne's Roman Catholic school was on Princes Street, just off King Street, and was a rather forbidding edifice of blackened stone, with the much newer church right beside it, flanked by Paradise Street, and with the parochial hall and the presbytery in the rear, on Paradise Lane. One morning in the summer of nineteen thirty-five, I joined the flow of children, adding my contribution to the endless clatter of clogs tramping and hurrying along the road, and happy and proud to be a schoolboy at last, a child no longer. With Jack on one side and my dad on the other, I could not have been happier, although I noticed several gloomy faces among my new fellows, and even the odd tear. This puzzled me, but as things turned out, the reason soon became clear.

Reaching the school gate, Jack released my hand and with a cheerful, 'See you at dinner time,' ran off towards the other gate. But when I made to follow, I was called back and my dad told me that Jack was now in the 'big lads' part, and I was to go into the 'infants.' What a shock, to be separated so quickly from Jack, and what a humiliation to be called an 'infant.' Hell, I was five years old. Well, nearly.

We walked down the narrow yard and into the school, and my dad took me into a classroom and plonked me down on a desk, with my feet on the seat of the desk in front, then went to the front of the classroom, where he held converse with a tall woman dressed from head to ankles in black, her bloodless face surrounded with a white wimple, and her pale eyes cold behind wire-framed glasses. Those eyes studied me closely as I perched on my desk-top and after a while, my dad left, with a smile and a wave of his hand. As soon as the door had closed behind him, Sister Margaret, as I soon found was her name and title, descended on me. I gazed up into her eyes.

'Sit properly,' she ordered. But as I was sitting already and comfortable enough, I merely continued to regard her thin features.

After a brief moment, when I hadn't complied, she leaned down, seized and lifted me by the arms and plonked me down onto the seat of the desk in front of me, with a force that made my teeth rattle.

'You sit on the *seat,*' she said, '*not* the desk-top.' And after imparting this piece of useful information, she returned to the large desk at the front of the class, and I began my first day at school.

Fortunately, Sister Margaret was not to be my regular teacher, but was merely filling-in for Miss Allen, a most charming lady who wore a floral housecoat and smelled of lavender, and from her I had my first lessons. We learned to count by means of a dog-eared board, divided into ten sections, each section bearing different coloured paper counters pasted on, ranging from one to ten. This wasn't too difficult, and neither was the alphabet, which was written in chalk on the blackboard, in both higher and lower case letters, which we wrote into our new exercise books with the pencils we had been issued with. I found I quite liked school, and when I met Jack at dinner-time, I was really proud, especially as I was now in the company of Jack's classmates, three years older than me, and members of the 'big lads' fraternity.

We tend, as we look back, to recall the good things and perhaps to magnify them, and I suppose there were as many bad days as good, but we get no pleasure from recalling those. However, facts are facts and there is no doubt that they were hard times. My dad got thirty-five shillings a week from the dole, and this was to pay the rent, insurance, food, fuel and clothing. It never stretched to a full week and there were times we sat in the firelight because we didn't have a penny for the gas meter.

In those days, we took a halfpenny to school each morning, if we had one, and for this we could choose between the one third of a pint of fresh milk or a cup of cocoa and an arrowroot biscuit. We often chose the latter because we had had no breakfast and the biscuit helped to stave off the hunger. On odd days, when we had the halfpenny and were *not* particularly hungry, we would spend the money at Cowell's sweet shop. The halfpenny would buy a two-ounce bar of chocolate or two ounces of sweets. Of course we never thought of ourselves as being poor; that thought never entered our heads because there were so many of us it was more or less the norm. The kids with good clothes and shoes, instead of clogs in winter or pumps in summer, were the exception that proved the rule. But if our pleasures and treats were few and far between, they were enjoyed all the more.

I gradually developed a love-hate relationship with St Anne's. It was an inevitable part of my life, and while I enjoyed learning, the sight of the grim old pile, especially on a raw, foggy winter morning when the lights were on in a vain attempt to combat the gloom, always caused a sinking sensation in my stomach. Many years later, when it was empty and awaiting demolition, like a condemned criminal awaiting the hangman, resigned and accepting, I would wander round from classroom to classroom, seeing and hearing the ghosts of teachers and boys. I would hear the stern commands of Mr Kent, or Mr Noblett or Mr Gregson; the furtive, whispered answers passed between desks when the teacher's attention was elsewhere, the dutiful laughter at the odd tutorial witticism, and the singing of the Latin hymns – O Salutaris Hostia, Tantum Ergo .....

I was never of a religious turn of mind, and later I developed a jaundiced view of all organised religion, feeling that it was merely a handy method of keeping people in check, and all of it based on fear rather than love; fear of what might happen to our immortal soul if we dared to question or challenge the dogma laid down by people who are, after all, merely mortal. But in spite of this, I always held the Roman Catholic Mass in high regard, for it was the one religion that was truly universal, and could be followed in any country on Earth. And because it was celebrated in a dead language, it could not be changed by the vagaries of fashion. I lost that respect when, faced with falling attendance, the Mass was changed to English in an obvious effort to keep hold of the waverers. A rock that is firmly bedded on the sea-bed does not shift with the tides.

One of the things I hated was the St Joseph's collecting card. These were squares of white card with a picture of St Joseph in the middle and a border of blank squares, twelve in all. The object was to find enough people willing to pay a penny for the privilege of making a hole with a pin in one of the squares. A full card meant a shilling collected, and this, and the card, had to be returned to the teacher as soon as possible.

There were, of course, many children in the area, and not too many spare pennies, and in a way, it amounted to begging, which was humiliating even to ragamuffins like me. Some of the non-Catholic neighbours were not above insulting us 'Papists,' and slamming the door in our faces. It was no fun to be one of the late starters in the tour of the streets, when every house you visited had already been tapped by one or more of your school pals and there would be nothing left for you. Sometimes, no amount of walking and calling on neighbours and relations would fill the card, and when we returned with squares unpricked, and less than the shilling, the teachers were often scathing in their remarks about lazy boys or apathetic Catholics.

The fact that our collecting was to provide shoes and clothing for 'poor' children in other parts of the world didn't help either, for most of the time we too were in dire need of footwear, especially in the winters, when the worst-off of all were grudgingly given chits to obtain a pair of clogs and most of our clothes were hand-me-downs and jumble-sale bargains. This was a charity that did *not* begin at home. The priest too, when he brought the cards to the school, would always be well-shod and wearing a good rainproof gabardine and gloves, while we often sat shivering with wet feet.

On Sundays, the priest would often denounce those who formed associations with non-Catholics, but they never queried the religion(s) of those who donated pennies to their funds, although many of them were those very same non-Catholics. I doubt they would have refused the contributions had they been informed, anyway. There are some things you can tolerate and some you can't.

Another fact of life was the pop-shop, and most people in our circle wore 'Indigo' clothes and shoes. The saying was that 'In-di-go on Monday and out-di-come on Friday,' with the few shillings borrowed on them seeing the people through the week, for even the thriftiest housewife found it impossible to spin out the dole money – and in some cases the *wages* – for a full seven days.

Jack and I took our turn at visiting 'Uncle Joe's', with its gas-lit, gloomy interior, its high counter (probably a deliberate policy to prevent irate customers leaping over to visit mayhem on the pawnbroker and his assistant), and the loft, with its racks of brown-paper parcels and the large square hatch from where the assistant dropped the redeemed articles to the pawnbroker on Fridays, and overall the sour smell of old, damp clothing. It was a depressing place to the adults who queued so patiently and hopefully with their meagre pawnables, but to me it was most interesting, and I wondered what it would be like to stand at the rail of the hatch and throw parcels down. I suppose I am lucky that I never had to do it, for the poor assistant worked horribly long hours in vile conditions for Cratchit-like wages, with the ever-present threat of picking up some of the lice and bed-bugs that must have infiltrated his dismal domain.

CHAPTER FOUR

Terriers and Teething Troubles

Dad had joined the 'Terriers,' (Territorial Army) the 4/5th Battalion of the East Lancashire regiment, one of the oldest infantry regiments in the army, and formerly known as the 30th Foot. It had served all over the globe, from the seventeenth century upheavals in the Lowlands, through the Napoleonic wars and the Crimea, the Great War of 1914-18, and on the Northwest Frontier. Arguably, it was the most battle-honoured regiment in the British army. One of the two regular battalions was always serving overseas, whilst the other occupied the 'Depot' at Fulwood Barracks in Preston.

This was 1933, when my father had been out of work for over a year, and in that twelve months, he had gone from optimistic job-seeking to philosophic acceptance of the dole as a permanent situation; or at least for the foreseeable future. At first, he had been dressed tidily enough, but without enough money to replace outworn items, he had gradually degenerated, like ninety per cent of his contemporaries, to second-hand and cast-off clothes. On the occasions when he reported for training at the Drill Hall on Canterbury Street, the transformation from down-at-heel unemployed labourer to ultra-smart soldier in sharply creased khaki, puttees and burnished boots, and with brasses glittering, was always a source of wonder to me.

On occasion, he would take me with him, and I soon grew to love the Drill Hall, the atmosphere of camaraderie amongst the men who drilled on the dusty square, so strong that even I could feel it. In the last years of the fragile peace, Dad had risen to the rank of sergeant, and I would stand enthralled as he drilled his platoon. The men, usually in their workaday clothes, sloping, ordering, presenting with the old Lee-Enfield Mk 3 rifles that had been standard issue in the first world war and had created confusion among the German forces with their rapid rate of fire and accuracy. A trained soldier could fire fifteen aimed rounds a minute. By the time I was eight years old, I could perform all of the drill movements and also 'fire' the Vickers machine gun, which they sometimes set up in the drill hall on wet days, with a print of a rural view on an easel, to teach the basics of such important things as identifying 'features,' calculating range, and arc of fire.

Those warm, late summer nights, with moths circling the electric lamp under the entry arch, and the voice of Gracie Fields floating over the dusty barrack square, are as vivid now as they were then:

> Little smile of welcome here,
> Little ray of sunshine there,
> Everyone is glad to see you
> Walking round the square ...'

On those warm evenings, especially with the music, there was always, for me at least, an air of 'Mad Carew' about the barracks, especially as one of the two regular battalions was serving in India. And if I tried hard, I could almost *see* the colonel's daughter crossing the dusty square. Some years ago, I called, out of pure nostalgia, and asked permission to look around. The adjutant kindly gave me permission and the run of the place, and as I walked into the drill hall, it was like stepping back half a century. I wouldn't have been in the least surprised to see some of the men I remembered; 'Cush' Cannon, Ernie Lightbown, Dick Grogan and many others. A door opened, and a man in civvies came out and asked who I was. When I explained, he became quite friendly and without any prompting on my part, told me quite seriously that the place was 'full of ghosts.' I can only say that I would have been very happy to see them.

Each year, during the summer, the battalion would go off to camp, to join one of the two regular battalions, and be brought up-to-date on weapons and tactics and that sort of thing. The 'camp' lasted for two weeks, and soon after he returned, looking fit and tanned, dad would be paid the bounty of five pounds. This was a wonderful time for us, because the bounty was in addition to the dole pay, as was the bonus. There would be new clothes and shoes for us, and for a week or two we would enjoy 'best' butter and a weekend roast, and sweets and picture money and all the other little things that some other families took for granted. It was soon gone, but while it lasted, we enjoyed it. I often think that the kids of today would benefit from a little dash of poverty; they would learn to appreciate the better days.

With the bounty money not yet spent, we would begin to take a penny every Monday morning, to be surrendered to the teacher and entered in our 'Penny Bank' books. The object was to save enough to provide a lump sum for the following year's holiday, but I don't think we ever got much more than a shilling or two saved before we needed to draw it out, and anyway, holidays were out of the question.

The 'infants' school finished a quarter of an hour before the 'boys,' and I used to go up and wait in the corridor until Jack came out. One day I was passing time by gripping the hinged side of the open cloakroom doorframe and levering myself forward, sliding on my smoothly-worn clog-irons on the red tile floor, when the bell rang and some boys dashed out and into the cloakroom. One of them, larking about, decided to close the door and keep his pal prisoner for a while. He didn't notice my fingers when he pulled the heavy oak door to, and fortunately, it didn't fit quite flush, or I would probably be typing this with one hand. I felt the door-edge tighten on my fingers, and for a moment, the shock of the pain stopped me uttering a sound, but then I let out a bellow and the boy, noticing me for the first time, released the door, which sprang back, so great had been the tension. Scarcely daring to look, I pulled my fingers out of the door-frame, just as the headmaster, Mr Kent, came striding along the corridor to see who was making this dreadful noise.

The skin on the backs of my fingers was like corrugated paper, with the raw flesh underneath beginning to bleed. I think I was too shocked and frightened to cry. Mister Kent grabbed me by the wrist and marched me to his study, where he opened the First Aid box and poured iodine over my fingers, and I found that I could cry after all. Quickly, he wrapped a cotton bandage around the injuries, and off I went, with Jack, a little sadder, a little wiser and a lot more tender.

The novelty of going to school had soon worn off, and I found that I didn't much care for it. We had to buy a catechism from the Catholic repository on King street, and every morning had to read and memorise some of it. I was disinterested and lazy with it, and had fallen far behind my classmates because of bouts of absence, a downward spiral which began with a visit to the school dental clinic on Victoria Street........

Our parents were ignorant of dental care and hygiene, and besides, brushes and paste were items that appeared, if at all, at the bottom of our list of priorities. Dad's dole money never even bought enough food, never mind luxuries. The result was that our teeth became decayed, and one molar in particular had been giving me sleepless nights, when one morning the dentist and nurse arrived and set up shop in Miss Wells' classroom. We were lined up, and went in, in turn, to sit in the chair and have our teeth checked and prodded and tapped with little hammers. The dentist muttered strange words to the nurse, who decoded them and marked a green card that showed a diagram of our teeth, with marks on certain ones. The molar which had been hurting me now bore a bold X, and the nurse handed it to me and told me to take it home and get it filled in by my mother or father.

I felt quite proud as I handed it over to my mother, and was a little puzzled by the sudden look of alarm she exchanged with my dad. The memory of Jack's treatment, having no less than six teeth extracted, was still fresh with them, although I knew nothing of it. Anyway, the tooth had to come out apparently, and so, reluctantly, she signed the card and I took it back to school.

A few days later, just after we returned from dinner, the teacher told me to go to the cloakroom, where my mother was waiting for me. Her eyes were sad as I got my coat, but for my part, it was a good day, for I had been told that I needn't return to school. 'Well,' I thought, 'a half-day holiday.' How I pitied my poor classmates who did not require dental treatment, poring over their books.

There was another boy getting his coat, and my mother asked him who was going with him, as she appeared to be the sole adult there. 'Nobody,' he said, and my mother, ever sympathetic to other peoples' troubles, took him under her wing and off we went through the town, the smell of hops from the brewery heavy on the air. I hated the smell of hops for many years, after that day.

Arriving at the clinic, mother realised she had forgotten the signed card, and the nurse, a fat Irish woman with the air and voice of a drill sergeant, gave her a bit of a roasting. I didn't like the look – or the sound – of this nurse, and just as I was wondering if this was going to be the treat I had anticipated, a shriek rang through the clinic, emanating from a room marked 'Surgery.' I caught a sudden fearful glance among the women and children gathered in the dismal waiting room. The sound unnerved me and I asked my mother what it was. She avoided my eyes as she explained that there was a boy with a badly cut knee, who was having his dressing changed, and the bandage was sticking. This somewhat reassured me, although I did wonder how my mother knew this, seeing that the boy must have already been in the surgery when we arrived. But of course, kids didn't question the wisdom of grown-ups.

The surgery door opened and a boy came out, crying quietly and holding a tiny rectangle of gauze to his mouth. I looked carefully at his knee, but could not detect a bandage. It must have been another boy, I thought. The nurse went into the surgery, the door closed, there was a murmur of voices, the door opened and my name was called. My mother rose too, and we went into the surgery, where another nurse beckoned me to a strange chair into which I dutifully climbed. As soon as I was settled, the dentist came over and told me to open my mouth wide. He lifted something that gleamed in the powerful overhead lights, while at the same time, I felt my wrists seized from behind.

The dentist's hand was icy cold as his fingers forced open my mouth a little further. And then something seemed to explode in my skull as the hypodermic syringe was inserted into the gum. The gum around the bad tooth was very tender and this sudden jab sent pain shooting up my face and made me cry out. My mother had refused to leave the surgery, to the annoyance of the dentist, and was sitting by the door, and I could just see, out of the corner or my eye, her anxious face as I struggled to get my wrists free.

'Be quiet,' snapped the dentist, a tall, gaunt man with wire-rimmed glasses. (Strange how so many cold-hearted people wore those - Sister Margaret, Mister Kent, and now this dentist).

He turned away, put down the syringe, and wrote briefly on a card, after which he picked up a silvery instrument and, again forcing my mouth open, put this thing in and I felt shock-pains of pure agony shooting through my jaw as he gripped the tooth. I shrieked far louder than the boy who had had his knee dressed.

'Don't be soft,' snapped the dentist, and this brought my mother to her feet in fury.

'Don't you call him soft,' she said, as he struggled with the tooth, and I struggled to free my wrists, and the nurse struggled to hold me. 'That tooth has been aching for twelve months, on and off, and it can't be numb in this time.'

He didn't answer, and with a final, angry wrench, had the tooth out, dropping it into a stainless steel basin. In the same fluid movement, he went to wash his hands, turning his back on my mother, who glowered at his back and at the nurse, who by now had released my wrists and instructed me to spit into the little whirlpool by the arm of the chair. She handed me a tiny square of gauze that was woefully inadequate for staunching the bleeding, and we were then shown out. The Irish nurse called out the name of the next victim, my schoolfellow.

Poor David. His teeth were in a terrible condition, and he was to have five removed. We sat and waited, me sobbing and holding the already sodden gauze to my mouth and my mother's face full of anguish for the kid in the surgery. But finally he was ushered out and we walked through the town centre, the subject of many glances, some sympathetic, others simply curious at this trio of a woman with an arm around each of two sobbing boys. The smell of hops still hung heavy in the air as we made our way to the dingy lodging-house where David lived, which was not far from either the school or the clinic. We went down a flagged passage to a room at the end, and there, like book-ends, either side of the fire, sat David's parents. My mother was furious at these two selfish people who were prepared to let the boy (David and I were still only five years old) face such a terrible ordeal alone, and she let them know in no uncertain terms. As for me, my mother kept me at home until the gum had healed, and I think this may have been the start of my reluctance to go to school.

And so I entered into a downward spiral; the more I avoided school, the further I got behind in learning, and the further I got behind, the more reluctant I was to go back. I had little trouble with the English and History and things, but was hopeless at Maths. I think that even had I never missed a day, I would never have been any good at maths; but I was even worse − if possible − with the catechism, and this was to teach me a salutary lesson in the near future.

One morning, the classroom door opened and the parish priest entered, and we all stood and chorused 'Good morning, father' as we had been taught. For some reason, the sight of a priest made me nervous, and on this particular morning, there was more reason than most, for he announced that he was here to carry out a catechism test. I nearly collapsed. Not next week, not tomorrow even, which would have given me a little time to swot up, but *now*. I would be found out for the lazy slacker I was, and would be held in scorn by my fellows. I shuddered to think what the reaction of Miss Kenyon would be - I had reluctantly graduated from Miss Allen's class that summer. And then my lively imagination conjured up a cunning plan. I sat stiffly and waited to put my scheme into action.

Smiling, the priest asked the first question, and my hand was reaching like Frank Swift's turning a Lawton header over the bar; demanding the right to answer, while my eyes shone with something closely akin to religious mania. The priest gave me the nod and I shot to attention like a fervent Nazi at a Nuremberg rally. The question was 'Who made you?' A simple, three syllable query, and the answer was equally simple and brief, 'God made me.' A smile, a nod and I sat down, mentally rehearsing the next answer, which I also knew. After that, I was lost. Came the question, and no-one else could have matched my response, and the priest, his smile now tinged with amusement and curiosity, and something else – perhaps caution or annoyance – nodded. I snapped to attention and belted out the answer and resumed my seat.

'Good, good,' murmured the priest, his eyes roaming over the rest of the field.

Question three, and this time, although my hand was quivering frantically – although I wasn't sure I knew the answer – I was passed over. And so it went on, for perhaps half an hour, with the priest ignoring my frantic wavings, and it was just as well, for I had long since run out of answers. Finally, the priest declared the exam finished, and himself well pleased. He congratulated Miss Kenyon on her charges' knowledge and enthusiasm, handed something to her and wished us all good morning and left. I felt drained, but my cunning plan had worked better than I had dared to hope.

Miss Kenyon told us that the priest had left some little tokens of his pleasure and those who had earned this recognition were to go to her and collect the token when she called their name. As each name was called, the boy or girl would go and receive a tiny medal with a hole through which could be passed a fine 'silver' chain - which could be purchased at the repository on King Street. Oh, there was a tidy measure of business acumen in the church that extolled the virtues of poverty. All the medals were gone, and although there was disappointment on some of the faces, I felt nothing but relief. I resolved to read the catechism and to memorise the answers, and ....

'There is a special prize here,' came the voice of Miss Kenyon, 'for the boy who showed most enthusiasm, and with whom Father Forrestal is very pleased.'

And she called my name.

Now this was really too much. I had deceived the poor priest and ought to have been punished rather than rewarded – and no doubt I would have been had he suspected – and as I went forward, I rather expected some sign of Divine displeasure. But nothing happened and Miss Kenyon handed me a small red prayer book. I suppose that was the moment when I should have owned up to my devilish deception and thrown myself on her mercy, but having witnessed several demonstrations of this, I kept my mouth firmly shut. Anyway, we were approaching time for our first Holy Communion and I was determined to do better after this let-off.

It was about this time that I engaged in my sole bout of fisticuffs. I can't remember the reason for the fight, or indeed, even the name of the lad. At the time, I was a keen Ken Maynard fan, and he tamed baddies without ever indulging in dirty tricks. Too naïve to appreciate that he fought to a script, I believed that justice would out, and when push came to shove with this snotty-nosed kid, I felt uncomfortable because he was perhaps a pound lighter than I was, and his small, mean eyes didn't quite mesh. I should have saved the pity for myself. He'd obviously never heard of Ken Maynard, and while I was busy adopting my pugilistic stance, he waded in with two large bony hands and two very fast feet. He knocked six bells out of me; I was hit simultaneously in the face, on the body and the shins so I didn't know what part to defend. The fight was broken up by Mr Gregson, who was on yard duty, and to whom I shall be forever grateful, but it convinced me that I was fit for neither the priesthood nor the prize-ring.

CHAPTER FIVE

A Journeyman Scholar

My mind was always prone to wandering during lessons, and often missed important bits of information. It was nothing I did deliberately; I just couldn't help it. I had improved with the catechism and had managed to more or less keep up with the others as regards attending Mass, and now we were seven years old, we were to make our First Holy Communion, having made our first confession the previous evening.

In happier, more affluent days, there had been a communal breakfast after this important ceremony, but times were hard, and we were told there would be no breakfast for us. We were exhorted to make an effort to wear white, dresses for the girls, shirts or blouses for the boys. But because of the Depression, we were told that those of us who did not own a white shirt or blouse or dress, could attend in their tidiest clothes, and the school would lend a white sash. This much I noted, as Miss Kent instructed us for this most important event. But then I suppose my mind began to wander, and when it returned to the classroom, I heard her saying that if anyone came late in the morning, and found the classroom empty, he or she was not to waste time, but to go straight into church. As I was often either late or only just in time, I made a firm resolution to be early. And I was. But when I reached the classroom, it was empty.

My empty stomach began to churn with fear, but, recalling Miss Kent's instructions, I hurried out of school and into church, puzzled that pupils were even then still arriving, which showed that I wasn't late. The church proved to be as empty as the classroom, and I made my way to the front pew as we had been told to do, and, after genuflecting, I slid onto the seat. A glance round told me that I was still alone, and I thought I'd better offer up a prayer, and dropped onto my knees, with a view to asking for divine help. Whether this worked is hard to say, but 'help' of a sort, was at hand.

I heard the swish of the door opening, and then there were footsteps approaching along the aisle. I could *hear* the suppressed anger in those tapping steps, which I knew instinctively were those of Miss Kent. The footsteps halted beside me and a small, cold hand gripped my left ear and pulled. I had no option but to follow it or part with it, and without even giving me time to genuflect, Miss Kent set off at a rate of knots, with me hobbling beside and slightly behind, my ear stretched to roughly twice its length and my head listing to starboard at a frightful angle.

We emerged to find ourselves facing a crowd of parents and other worshippers who were waiting for our procession to enter the church. It was humiliating and rather painful as Miss Kent marched me back into the school and into *Miss Wells'* classroom, where the other communicants had gathered. This change of meeting-place was the little bit of information my wandering mind had missed. Roughly, Miss Kent thrust a white sash over my shoulder and dragged my arm through, and then we formed up into two lines, one of boys and one of girls. Joining hands piously, we walked with downcast eyes through the narrow yard and into the church. An hour or so later, we returned our sashes and had the rest of the day off. I can't honestly say I felt any different for having received the Sacrament, but no doubt that was my fault entirely, for the teachers and priests certainly did their best to hammer religion into us. They must have succeeded with most, but I never felt I had a vocation.

After I had made my First Communion, I moved up to the 'big boys' school. This would be following the summer holiday of 1938, about the time of the Munich Crisis, although such things didn't worry us kids. The main thing was, I was now in the same school as Jack, feeling very grown up and superior, especially when we were issued with real pens, not pencils, and real thick text-books rather than the thin ones we'd learned from as infants.

I was never very keen on playtime, when six or seven classes of boys were released from the classrooms to let off steam for fifteen minutes. The yard became a veritable madhouse of football games, cowboys chasing Indians, cops apprehending robbers, future businessmen trading, and groups engaged in games played with cigarette cards and marbles, while the non-stop rattle of clogs formed a backing to the screams, shouts and laughter.

Some of the more introverted boys would seek out quiet spots and read the current Dandy or Beano, or one of the big four, Hotspur, Adventure, Wizard or Rover. The teachers, as a rule, tended to frown on the stories. Whether they were of a 'Six-gun Gorilla' who roamed the American West in search of the killers of his master – who had taught him never to waste ammunition (!) – striding across the title-page like a miniature King Kong, firing his twin revolvers into the air (which seemed to negate the frugal teaching of his late master), or the wielder of the famous 'Clicky-Bah' (cricket bat, to those poor uninformed non-readers) who enjoyed a different adventure every week on the North West frontier. As the wielder was a young Indian, one would have expected that he found little difficulty in pronouncing his 'R's and 'T's, but there you are; logic didn't play too big a role with either the writers or readers. The tales were *enjoyable* and that was all we demanded, and characters, like the Indians Ram Jam Phul and Ransid Buttah, made our ribs ache with laughter.

Perhaps they took a more tolerant view of the school stories, either of the fat owl of Greyfriars, Billy Bunter, or the devious Alfred Smugg of Red Circle. But these tales always took second place to Baldy Hogan the footballer, and Wilson, the aesthetic athlete who was built like a street lamp and wore an all-in-one suit of black that could have been winter underclothing or the latest designer-wear for the bleak Yorkshire moors, his habitat. Despite his build – or lack of it – he could run the almost-four-minute mile, out-sprint a Cheetah. and lift weights that would have broken the spirit the greatest super-heavy weightlifter. They don't write 'em like that anymore, and the lads of today are the worse for it.

Miss McKenna ruled her class with a rod, not of iron, but of pliable cane. She was the sole female teacher in the 'boys' school, and was respected and feared just as much as her male colleagues – with the possible exception of the headmaster, Mr Kent. She rewarded good behaviour and bad and there was nothing 'politically correct' in her sentencing and execution. Indeed, the teachers of those days enjoyed an authority that would be the envy of today's oppressed tutors. They were days of obedience and discipline, and punishment was endorsed all the way up to the government, so no-one complained too loudly at the odd hiccup, but merely accepted that no system was perfect and that mistakes were possible. And of course, we all – pupils, teachers, and parents – benefited from this discipline. With it one can do anything, without it, nothing. For good behaviour, or honest endeavour and diligence, the reward was a toffee lollipop, while the reward for bad behaviour was one or two strokes of the cane; and for all her femininity, she wielded a mean cane, as I soon learned.

'I am going out for a moment,' she announced one morning, 'and while I am away, you will get on with your work and be quiet. When I return, I want to be able to hear a pin drop.'

This was all the warning she needed to issue, and when she had uttered it, out she went, closing the door quietly behind her. For a while, silence reigned, but with thirty or so boys, there were always some who had either more courage or less sense than the majority, and this class had just one. When a few minutes had passed, he began to whisper to someone, despite the chorus of 'shhh's' from the silent majority. He persisted, not exactly talking, but in loudly whispering.

The door – like that of the Malamute Saloon - flew open with a crash, and there stood Miss McKenna, eyes narrowed and mouth grim as she stepped to her desk. At that moment, I think a falling pin would have shattered my eardrums, but it was too late.

'Come out the boy who was talking,' she said.

Needless to say, nobody moved. We all knew who it was, but of course, there was a code of honour that had to be respected, and so we remained silent as her sharp eyes roamed the room, like Gagool conducting the Witch-Hunt in ' King Solomon's Mines.'

'Very well,' she stated flatly, 'if the guilty boy does not own up, I will cane the whole class.'

This bald statement of intent sent shock-waves pulsing through my body, for I was in pole position, at the front and left of the class, and I began to send frantic mental messages that appealed to the whisperer, to the effect that he was bound to be caned anyway, so why not do the decent thing and spare the rest of us. Especially me. Obviously we were on different wavelengths, or he was paralysed by fear, for he remained mute and still. Which, ironically, had he been so while she was out, would have avoided all this unpleasantness.

She waited a few seconds, then reached for her cane and advanced on me.

'Stand up.'

I rose to my feet.

'Hold out your hand.'

She raised the thin cane high, there was a swish and a sudden burning sensation across my fingertips, followed immediately by a painful throbbing. I made to sit, but she had other ideas.

'Now the other one.'

After the second stroke, I was permitted to sit while she worked her way along the apprehensive rows, and I could feel tears pricking my eyelids while my fingertips burned and throbbed, but I suppose it was best to be first, although her arm was strongest, for I would not have enjoyed sitting and waiting. Of course, we bore no malice for this 'overcane.' It was accepted. The guilty had to be punished, and when the guilty one was unidentified, this was the only way to be sure he *was* punished. Things balanced out – for me, at any rate – when, a few days later, I was instructed to go the cupboard and help myself to one of the lollipops that she kept in a large box.

CHAPTER SIX

Gas Masks and Gardening

War was in the air. Chamberlain had gone off to make his obeisance's to Hitler and in the meantime, we watched gangs of men building air-raid shelters and filling sandbags from the sandhills in Pleasington playing fields, the venue for so many field days in happier times. My dad brought home and studied training manuals, and activity at the Drill Hall increased. We had to go to Bank Top school on West Street, to be issued with gas-masks and be instructed on their fitting and wearing by Mr Croasdale, the Air

Raid Warden. It was all excitement and great fun for us kids, especially the boys, and the groups gathering in the club doorway or under the gas-lamp at the bottom of Pink Street now talked of bombers and anti-aircraft guns and barrage balloons instead of football and cricket.

And then it all collapsed into nothing, when Chamberlain returned with his scrap of paper. It was certainly not peace for our time – well, at least, not for much of it – but it was a breathing space. In the meantime, there was trouble on a minor scale at home, and I was the centre of it.

I don't rightly remember what caused the rift, but my parents, especially my mother, had been concerned by my constant refusal to go to school. I didn't so much refuse, as put on acts, and I am not proud of the way I pulled the wool over my mother's eyes by feigning illness. There were few complaints I couldn't fake when I wanted to avoid school. I saw things only as a child, and it was only very much later in life that I saw her side of the coin, the worry that I was genuinely ill, the frequent visits by the Schools Attendance Officer, and, in the end, the summons to appear before a Committee, to explain my all-too-frequent absences.

It may have been a state of ongoing fear engendered by the dental clinic, or it may have been the fact that I often missed Mass and was so far behind with the strict religious training that I was just terrified of going. Or it may have been a combination of all of these things, coupled with the harsh regime which was magnified by my fertile imagination until I was sometimes physically sick as nine o'clock approached. It was certainly a downward spiral and my mother was at her wits end. So much so that one day she made her decision, a most unpopular one with her staunch –even bigoted – family, but one which I welcomed avidly. I would leave St Anne's and go to Bank Top council school.

And I did, and I enjoyed my few years there in a manner I would have thought impossible before.

In the summer of 1937, my dad's sister, Aunt Lizzie, and Uncle Bill (Higginbotham), moved into number 25 Pink Street, with their two boys, our cousins Jack, a few months younger than my brother

Jack, and 'Little' Bill, a few months younger than me. They both attended Bank Top Council school so one morning, about the start of the conker season, my dad took me down to the school and I was placed in Mrs Butler's class. And how different it all was. Mrs Butler was an elderly, sweet-natured woman who had a keen sense of humour and understood children very well. She was an altogether lovely lady, I liked her immensely, and in her class I began to show my true potential for learning.

We gathered in the Hall for morning prayers, and I learned that the Church of England's version of the 'Our Father' was a little different than the Roman Catholic version. Neither did we make the sign of the cross, but apart from these things, and the absence of Sacred Hearts and Madonnas in the classrooms, things were much the same.

'They won't teach him anything wrong,' my mother had told Aunt Gert, when she was being castigated for taking me away from the Roman Catholic faith. Nor did they, I really enjoyed going to school, and my mother had no further trouble. As for myself, well, I was neither better nor worse for the shift, but infinitely happier.

By this time, Jack had left St Anne's for St Alban's Higher Grade school, and Joan, now five years old didn't want to continue at St Anne's, so my mother let her go to Bank Top, and she too was happy there. All in all, it was a good school.

One Friday dinner-time, when I came home from school, my mother told me that dad was gone.

Where? I wanted to know, and was told that the 4/5th had been mobilised, because the Germans had invaded Poland and now war was inevitable. I can't recall being particularly upset, for we were used to dad going off for weekend camps, and for the annual summer camp, so really, it was no big deal for us kids, although obviously it was for my mother. She would be alone now, with two half-grown, boisterous lads on her hands and a country at war to cope with.

She, of course, remembered the Great War, with its tragedies and heartaches, but we were still blithely innocent, and to be honest, I think we boys were actually looking forward to it, believing it would be rather like the Hollywood versions we had seen, and disillusionment was still quite a long way off.

Large areas of the town were taken over for the growing of vegetables, and some schools were allotted land in Griffin Park. The headmaster, Mr. Sudworth, was a very keen and capable gardener, and with the help of the bigger boys, had soon cleared the grass from our patch and we dug and double-dug and planted potatoes, peas, onions, leeks, carrots, Brussels sprouts, and cauliflowers. The 'plot' soon became one of my favourite periods, and under the guidance of Mr. Sudworth, we weeded, thinned out, earthed up and tended the soil with fertilisers and phosphates. We learned to clean and oil all the tools, which we kept in the former stables of Griffin Lodge, which we shared with two 'pumps' of the newly-formed Auxiliary Fire Service and their crews.

One December morning, as we assembled for morning prayers, Mr Sudworth, looking more excited than was his wont, informed us that the German pocket battleship Graf Spee had been sunk by British ships, and we cheered wildly, although, to be honest, most of us didn't really appreciate the situation.

We had our first wartime Christmas party, and although the windows were criss-crossed with strips of gummed paper to minimise flying glass in the event of a bomb landing nearby, we enjoyed ourselves tremendously. I was asked to draw a caricature of Hitler, so we could play a version of putting the tail on the donkey, with blindfolded pupils trying to pin a moustache on the dictator's top lip. And, as most older people will no doubt remember that first wartime winter, we had one of the heaviest snowfalls on record. Some outlying villages like Guide, Belthorn and Brinscall were cut off, their inhabitants having to leave their houses via the bedroom windows, the snow having drifted so high. At the party, Jack Slater sang a song for us:

    Does a lamp-post get bronchitis in the winter
    Standing on the corner of the street?
    When it's wet and windy, and he starts to cough?

Does the little mantle in his globe fall off?
He hasn't got an overcoat or nightie,
To cover up his poor cold feet,
Does a lamp-post get bronchitis in the winter
Standing on the corner of the street?

In March, we received a field-card from dad, who was 'Somewhere in France' with the 4th Battalion, which was part of the British Expeditionary Force under Lord Gort. It was the period of the 'Phoney War,' but all that ended at dawn on the tenth of May, when, from that first onslaught, the BEF, divided and disrupted, was retreating piecemeal to Dunkirk, despite many small resistances which stopped the German is their tracks here and there. During one of these delaying actions, Captain Irvine-Andrews, of the East Lancs, won the army's first VC of the war.

Everyone remembers the long, hot summer of 1940. The soldiers who had been evacuated from the beaches of France were already tanned from the heat of the sun, and the tattered, unshaven, unwashed, red-eyed man who came into our house and dropped his rifle in the corner was no exception.

The last time I had seen Dad in uniform, he had been, as usual, smartness itself, in the pre-war khaki tunic, peaked hat and puttees. But this scarecrow was in torn battle-dress, his boots dusty and worn right through. His rifle had a curious groove across the butt, where, as I later discovered, a German bullet had struck at the very instant he leaped over some obstacle. Perhaps if he had not jumped, the bullet would have either killed or wounded him. He was so weary, he fell asleep with a mug of tea in his hand, and after going to bed, even in the stifling heat, he slept for fourteen hours.

He had been granted only 48 hours leave, and when that was up, he reported to (I think) Squires Gate holiday camp which had been taken over by the army, and where the regiment was reforming. There were plans to convert the 4th into an armoured battalion, and so the older members and those not fully fit were weeded out and posted to other units. This plan was later abolished. Dad, who was nearly forty, and quite old to be a fighting soldier, was detached to the South Wales Borderers, as Permanent Staff Instructor to units of the Welsh Home Guard. My mother heaved a sigh of relief that he had been given a safe billet. As things turned out, it was far from safe, but that was to come later.

CHAPTER SEVEN

Grief, Grammar-School and Grants

Little Bill was a wonderful playmate. As he and I were so close in age and temperament, we were much nearer brothers than cousins, and he and I got on from the first. He was generous and altogether the very epitome of what a pal should be. Uncle Bill, like so many of our dads, had joined the Terriers in the thirties, and was now 'Somewhere In England.'

All through that long summer, we followed the exploits of Fighter Command, relishing the real-life exploits of Paddy Finucane and Bob Stanford-Tuck, and collecting Dinkie toys of Wellingtons, Blenheims, Spitfires and Hurricanes.

On one sweltering day, a gang of us trekked to Samlesbury aerodrome to see what we could of the planes that sometimes flew quite low over the town. We somehow found the aerodrome, which was quite an achievement, as we never really had any idea of the whereabouts of places, and therefore could not formulate any travel plans. And so we were thrilled beyond words to catch sight, over the boundary hedge and fence, of a Hurricane taxiing along the perimeter track. But we were moved on by a sour-faced Air Ministry policeman with a rifle slung over his shoulder. What the hell he thought we were doing, I can't imagine, unless he thought we were a group of German agents cunningly disguised as British schoolboys. But we'd reached our goal and achieved our aim, and even the cloudburst that drenched us in our shirt-sleeves and pumps failed to take the edge off this wonderful day.

Autumn came and we harvested our crops, which were sold cheaply to parents and relations and were very well-received, especially the onions, because, for some reason, they had been in very short supply and had even become the subject of comedians' wit. The one pest that defied Mr Sudworth's expertise was the wireworm. These fine insects could burrow their way right into the heart of the potatoes, and many a fine-looking spud was found to have the pest well-ensconced, although it never put anyone off.

As the winter advanced, we dug the ground over and prepared it for the following spring. By March we were happily planting again. We were a very happy band of young 'plotters' and as the year advanced, up came the crops – and the weeds. Couch grass and dandelions seemed to grow overnight and we were hard put to keep them in check. The fact that we were able to do so made me realise the truth of the proverb 'Many hands make light work.'

That summer of 1941 was a bad time for me, and even now, I cannot recall the event that caused me so much pain without my eyes growing misty. Little Bill had caught an infection and was confined to bed. The doctor had visited, but didn't seem unduly concerned, and Aunt Lizzie thought it must be the 'flu.' We were out playing at the bottom of Pink Street. It was a bright but breezy July day and we were taking turns to ride cousin Jack's bike, when all at once, some inner voice told me to go and see how Billy was.

When I went into their house, there was no-one downstairs, so, calling Aunt Lizzie's name, I went up to the back bedroom. Billy lay in bed, his cheeks rosy with fever and his eyes closed. He seemed to me to be sleeping peacefully, but Aunt Lizzie was stroking his brow and talking softly to him, my mother and Mrs Ashley, a neighbour, were in the room. Billy seemed to be breathing shallowly, and with difficulty, and Mrs Ashley produced a tiny bottle of brandy.

'Give him a drop of this,' she said, but the liquid just dribbled down Billy's chin.

Aunt Lizzie soaked a cloth in cold water, folded it, and placed it on his forehead. All at once, Billy's eyes rolled upwards until only the whites showed, and in that hot little room, with the dust-motes dancing in the sunbeams, the quiet rasping of his breathing suddenly stopped. My mother and Mrs Ashley began to cry quietly, although Aunt Lizzie – who was very deaf and may not have been aware of any change – carried on talking softly to him and stroking his forehead. After a while, my mother said, 'He can't hear you, Lizzie,' and I knew he was dead. Little Bill. The best and kindest friend a boy could have had. I cried then and I mourn now, sixty years on.

Some people grumbled about the rationing, but our family were better fed than we had been before the war. For one thing, we were forced to eat healthily, and for another, Dad's army allowance was at least twice as much as the dole money, and with him being away, there were only four mouths to feed. I grew to like Mondays, for that was the day my mother drew the allowance and bought in the rations, so there would be tea, butter, sugar, bacon, cheese etc., and there would be money for the King's Hall, whose Programme changed twice weekly, on Monday and Thursday. Whether we'd have the money for the Thursday programme was always iffy, but on Monday we were sure of it.

In the early summer of 1942, I sat the second part of the 'Scholarship' exam. Two of us from Bank Top had passed the first part, and we had to go to St Peter's C-of-E school on Byrom Street for the second part.

It was a beautiful day, and when Jack Slater and I arrived, the yard was full of boys from many different schools, all there to sit the exam, apart from the school's own complement. We were ushered into a classroom, where tables were set out with blotting paper and inkwells and pens, and on the stroke of nine, the first papers were handed out, and we began. There was no talking, the invigilator patrolling between the rows to make sure no cribbing went on, and we sat in that hot, dusty room from nine until twelve, with no break for playtime. It was hard to listen to the sound of boys playing football and cricket while we dipped our pens and chewed the end, and racked nervous brains. But noon came at last and off we went for a much-needed break. In the afternoon, it was a repeat, and by the time the final papers were collected and we were allowed out, I was drained. But it all seemed worth while when the results were published in the Blackburn Times, for we both had passed, and had been awarded 'free' places at Queen Elizabeth's Grammar School, where all the rich kids went.

The Blackburn Times was published on Friday, and on the following Monday, at assembly, Mr Sudworth made the announcement to the whole school. He was very proud that two boys from his small school had won such prestigious places, and called us up to the dais, where he presented each of us with a sixpence. A few weeks later, when we broke up for the summer holiday, I felt real regret that I would not be returning after the break. I had been at Bank Top for only three years, but I loved the place and liked and respected the teachers. I think I would have been more than happy to stay on until the official elementary leaving age of fourteen, but that was not possible, as all the eleven-plus pupils had to leave for secondary education.

Towards the end of the holiday, a boy in Queen Elizabeth's Grammar School uniform called at our house one evening, and left a large envelope. There was great excitement as my mother opened it, but the excitement soon turned to despair when she read from the list of things I must have to take my 'free' place:

Blazer, with badge, which must be from one of only two
shops on the list,
Raincoat or overcoat, ditto,
Grey flannel trousers, short or long,
Cap, with badge, ditto,
Stockings,
Black shoes (No clogs or pumps or wellingtons at QEGS)
Straw hat,
Football kit,
Cricket strip, (Flannels, white shirt and cricket boots),
PT kit, and a load of other things,
Certain books that were not supplied,
Drawing instruments
and God knows what else.

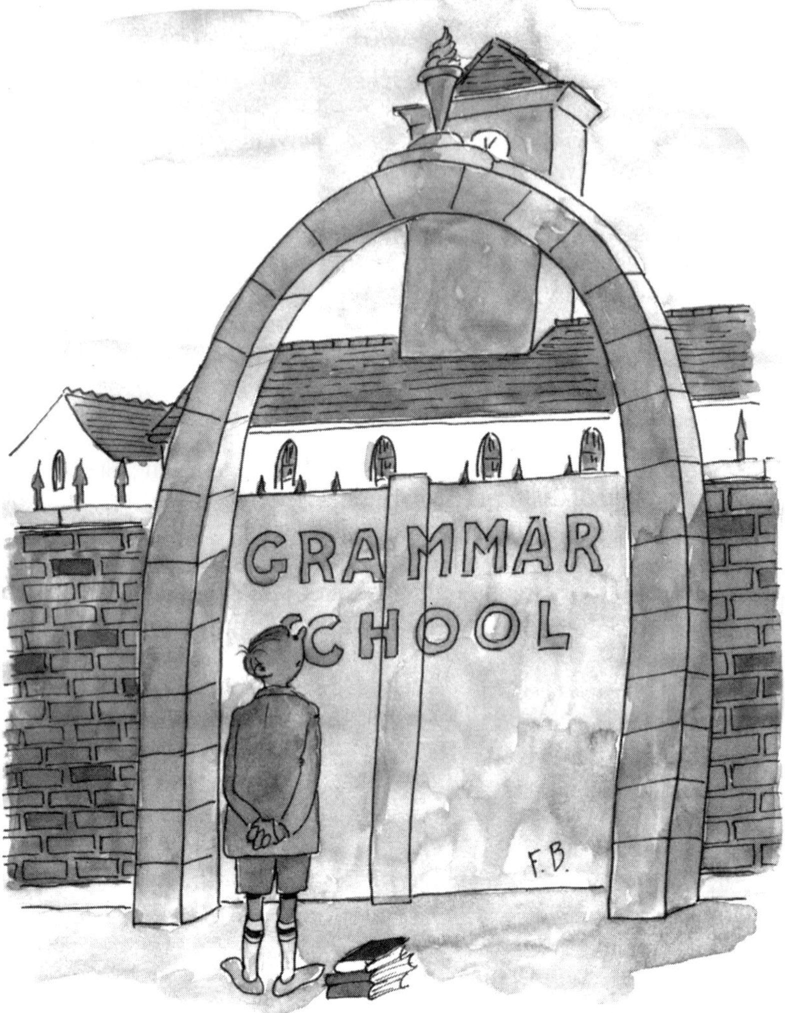
GRAMMAR
CHOOL
F.B.

There was no way we could get them. Some neighbour, hearing of our problem, told my mother that she had heard there was a grant available for parents who couldn't afford these things, and my mother duly applied to, I think, the Education Office. She was turned down. Perhaps it was because my abysmal attendance at St Anne's had been brought to their notice and they were unwilling to invest money in higher education for such a risky pupil. Whatever the reason, my 'free' place – and the grant, so we heard – went to the son of a town councillor. I can't say whether this was true or not, but that was the story that found its way to our house, and the fact remains that *somebody* got a place he hadn't won. But as Bunyan says, he that is down need fear no fall, and what I never had, I never missed.

When school resumed, I was found a place at Blakey Moor Secondary Modern school. After St. Anne's and Bank Top, this was, to me, rather like Red Circle in the comics, even having its own Mr Smugg. Some of the masters wore gowns and we had a different teacher for each lesson; not like my two former schools, where one teacher taught his or her class in all of the lessons. I quite liked Blakey Moor at first, but I hadn't been there a year when I renewed acquaintance with the school clinic – *not* the dental department, but something not far short of it in terms of trauma.

We had had our vision tested and my left eye was thought to be 'lazy.' So one day I had to attend the clinic for a further eye test. Now I was always very wary of things being done to my physical body, especially after the tooth business, and as no-one bothered to explain what was going to be done, I was on edge when I attended. My name and school were duly recorded and I was told to sit on a bench and wait with the others in the dismal waiting room. After a while, a nurse – not the one of fond dental memory, but another Irish woman with piercing eyes and hands like number ten spades, a feature I eyed askance with memories of being held captive in the dentist's chair – called my name and I was ushered into the treatment room.

There was another weird-looking chair here, and another man in white, who ordered me to sit. I climbed onto the chair and the nurse pushed my head back against the headrest and forced one of my eyes open. Before I could blink, something dropped into it, something that immediately began to smart with an intensity that brought tears, and made me shut my lids tightly. My first thought was that some awful mistake had been made, and that the stuff that was now burning my eyeball could only be some form of acid that would blind me. But before I could move, the other lid was forced open and in went the drops, after which I was allowed to get up from the chair and told to return to the waiting room. I stumbled out, unable to see for the tears. It was like the effect you get from peeling strong onions, but much worse. And when I finally managed to keep my eyes open, I found, to my horror, that everything was blurred.

If someone had taken the trouble to explain that the drops were designed to dilate the pupil, so that the optician could better find the correct lenses, all might have been well. But not one word had been spoken, and my wild imagination was doing its best to convince me that this was the onset of total blindness, deliberately visited on me by this diabolical optician and nurse. And when I was ordered to return for a second dose, I was off.

I made it as far as the door, and had it half open, when I was grabbed by the wrist and hauled back by my mother, who had been told to accompany me.

'Wait until I see Mr Street,' (the headmaster) said the nurse, as I was thrust into the chair and given the treatment again. 'I'll tell him what a great big softie you are.'

Back on the bench, I was now resigned to being blind, and the third and final treatment brought forth no reaction. I couldn't focus on anything at all; the faces of the other victims were merely lightish blobs in the dismal little room, but I took a little comfort from the presence of my mother. If she was accepting this, it must be all right. Perhaps she had been informed that I wouldn't be able to see properly, and that was why she had to go with me, but even she had not sought to quiet my alarm.

Into the treatment room again, and this time I was fitted with something like a pair of spectacles, but with slotted half-circles in place of lenses. The optician began to fit various lenses into the slots, asking me if I could see clearly, while he peered into my eyes. And to my amazement, I found I *could* see very clearly, and the fear that I would be permanently blind began to recede. After trying perhaps a dozen lenses, he seemed satisfied and the nurse removed the spectacles, which threw everything out of focus again, and my mother was given a form and we left. Outside, the late afternoon sun had come out and was glinting off the wet pavement – it had rained heavily earlier – and I couldn't keep my eyes open because of the glare. I was completely disoriented and would never have got home alone.

I had been given a small card and told to take it to school and show it to my teacher, as I wouldn't be able to do any 'close work' for a few days. Now this was fine by me, having got over the initial trauma of impending blindness, and I used that card for about three weeks, long after my vision had returned to normal. The worst thing was that, when I got home, the lads were playing football at the bottom of the street. I managed to grope my way down, but couldn't see the ball, and so had to sit out the game.

CHAPTER EIGHT

Return To St Anne's, via Blackamoor

I had been at Blakey Moor less than a year when a routine medical inspection gave the examining doctor cause for concern. I was flat-chested, and with TB still not extinct, there were fears that I might have contracted this disease. A few years previously, Maggie Duxbury, the nineteen year old elder sister of my childhood playmate, had died from TB. I had to attend the Duke Street clinic for tests, but these proved inconclusive, and a few weeks later, my mother had to take me to Queen's Park hospital for further tests.

This must have been a very worrying time for my mother, with my dad away and all the hardships of life in wartime to face, apart from this. Fortunately, the tests proved negative, but the medical authorities decided to send me to the Open Air school at Blackamoor for a while, and I was quite happy about this as my sister Joan was already a pupil there and liked it tremendously.

As we caught a bus from Griffin, that first morning, I felt a little embarrassed to be under the guidance of my little sister, but soon got into the routine. First the bus to the Boulevard, and then onto one of the three special buses that waited each morning beside the Palace cinema. After a nice, long, uphill ride, we alighted at the gates of the school, which was set in fields at the foot of Fishmoor Reservoir. It was somehow similar to Bank Top Workingmen's Club in that it was of dark red rustic brick with green slate roofs and cream coloured window frames and doors.

Here, the accent was on health rather than academic brilliance. First thing, we drank our free milk, then, in the middle of the morning, monitors brought round huge jars of cod-liver oil and malt and a bowl full of teaspoons and we all had a spoonful. I quite enjoyed this, and sometimes managed an extra spoonful, for some of the kids hated it and were always glad of a pal who would take it for them. After that it was outside into the fresh air for about fifteen minutes, and at twelve noon, we marched into the dining room to the strains of a rousing march, thumped out with great enthusiasm by Miss Pickstone on the upright piano.

The staff at Blackamoor did a wonderful job of feeding us, and I put on weight and felt altogether better. After dinner, we got our camp-beds from the annexes at the end of the sheds, and rested for an hour, some with blankets, some with sleeping bags, while one of the teachers sat and read a book. The hour up, we put away the beds and spent ten or fifteen minutes on the playing field, then back to lessons for about an hour, another period of play, and then the last lessons of the day, after which bus tickets were issued for use on the Corporation buses. At four o'clock, we got on the three special buses waiting for us at the gates and were taken back to the Boulevard, where Joan and I caught the Cherry Tree bus to Griffin. This was the sort of school I had always wanted and I think I liked it better than Bank Top; certainly I liked the routine better.

Union shirts were the sort that men wore for their warmth and hardwearing qualities, and Uncle Anthony (O'Neill), Aunt Gert's husband, always wore them. Of their hardwearing quality there could be no doubt, for when the sleeves had worn through at the elbows, the body, with it's warm half-lining, was still good. And when she bought new ones, Aunt Gert would bring the old ones down to our house and my mother would cut out the sleeves entirely. Then in winter, I would wear the shirt under my jersey. The snag was, Uncle Anthony was about twice my chest size, so when we stripped for PT, I was too embarrassed to remove the jersey on its own, and doffed the two garments together, which, as our wardrobe didn't run to vests, left me naked to the waist. To add to my embarrassment, Miss Wilkinson would say 'Look at Burns, the stalwart.' (This on a raw frosty morning when most of the lads were pleading to be allowed to keep their shirts on). 'Not even keeping his vest on. Doesn't he make you feel ashamed?'

Of course I didn't make them feel ashamed, but if they or Miss Wilkinson had known the reason for my stalwartness, I certainly would have been.

Sometime during the summer of 1943, there was a competition for designs for a 'green belt' area, something on which the government of the day was very keen. Now I didn't know what the hell they meant by a green belt, but I had a little talent for drawing, and when we got the papers, I drew a small estate of council houses, with a bowling green and little park area, or something like that. At the time, I don't think I quite knew what a council house looked like, but I must have struck a chord with someone at the Town Hall, for I was awarded first prize, and the Mayor came up to the school to present it. I believe it was Miss Wilkinson who donated it out of her own pocket. It was a drawing block and four pots of poster colours and a small book outlining the basics of cartooning, and if the drawing paper was of poor wartime quality, it certainly didn't detract from the pleasure. Miss Wilkinson was a lovely lady, always kind and thoughtful, and later became headmistress of the school. There could not have been a better choice.

Because of the nature of the school, there were some Roman Catholic pupils, and every morning Mr Kent, from St Anne's, came to take religious instruction for about half an hour. If he remembered me, he gave no indication. We used to gather, about fifteen of us, in the dining hall immediately after drinking our morning milk, and were instructed in my old stumbling-block, the catechism. We said our Catholic prayers, had a bit of a pep-talk, and then he left and we carried on with our normal lessons. I suppose, strictly speaking, I ought not to have been included, as I had not attended a Catholic school for five years, but no-one mentioned this and I wasn't bothered one way or the other.

The winter of 1943 was a bad one for us, especially me. I had caught a bad dose of 'flu' and to complicate things, I also got pleurisy. To make things just that bit worse for my mother, we had had a fire in the loft, caused by smouldering soot getting through a space where a couple of bricks had fallen out of the chimney breast. Part of the ceiling had had to be knocked out, leaving a gaping hole, and until it was fixed, we couldn't light a fire. So when I went down with illness, I had to be put into poor grandma Bamford's bed. As she couldn't climb, it had been brought downstairs, and she slept as best she could in her rocking chair before the fire, which she kept burning night and day. Grandma's life was one of hardship and sacrifice and we children never realised just how much we owed to her. When she died, at the age of eighty one, she had never known the luxury of a carpet, or even of cheap linoleum. If the poorest on earth is the richest in Heaven, then she is now very rich indeed.

I must have been very ill, for I recall once waking up, (I must have been unconscious, rather than sleeping), to find my mother crying beside the bed. No doubt she was remembering Little Bill. But, although I was confined to bed for about three weeks, I recovered, and the men came and mended the ceiling and I moved back home. Those wartime days, especially in the long dark months of winter, with the blackout in force, were bleak and depressing. Even the Christmases were austere, with all kinds of ingenious substitutes for the proper Christmas fare.

In April 1944, there was a dispute between the school authorities and the Roman Catholic faction. I don't really know the ins and outs, but I think the school people claimed that the thirty minutes visit of Mr Kent somehow disrupted the curriculum. The upshot was that the Catholic authorities ordered all the Catholic children to return to their schools. Obviously they considered the soul more important than the body, and so with great reluctance, I returned to St Anne's. I had been a maverick for five years, with a most patchy education taken in fits and starts, and here I was, with less than a year to go, back at the seat of my original trouble. Still, I was well enough received by most of the lads I remembered, Mike Moran, Tommy Gannon, Alec Furey and others and I think that if I had applied myself, I could have made up a lot of lost ground. But I was lazy and uninterested.

Mr Kent was on yard duty. When he blew the first blast on his whistle, the clamour ceased at once, and everyone stood still, as if playing the old game of 'Statues.' On the second blast, we formed into lines by class. I was in the senior class, with the other thirteen-year-old pupils. We shuffled and sorted ourselves out under the jaundiced eye of Mr Kent, on whose lantern-jawed face I never saw a smile, and then we waited for the third blast, which would be our cue for marching into school. Suddenly, Mr Kent's finger pointed at me, and he said, in his clear, dry voice, 'Francis, go up to my room and wait for me.'

Now normally, this was bad news, for that phrase meant, 'when I'm ready, I'll come and knock hell out of you.' We were never told what the infringement was, and of course we never asked. But I knew I had done nothing wrong, so I wasn't particularly worried, even when my classmates, filing past, demonstrated their glee and made bloodcurdling estimates on the number of stripes. If there was one thing that puzzled me, though, it was the use of my Christian name. I was, and always had been 'Burns,' never 'Francis.' One by one, the columns filed into their classrooms and a silence fell. It seemed to stretch on for ever, but was eventually broken by the unhurried scrape of Mr Kent's shoes ascending the worn stone stairs. He opened his door and beckoned me in, and as I did so, I closed the door behind me. Mr Kent turned to stare at me, his pale eyes cold behind the wire-framed glasses.

'It wasn't you I told to come up ' he said, ' but the boy behind you, Francis Baldwin. He was fidgeting.'

Well, this explained everything, of course. First of all, how could I know who was immediately behind me? I didn't have eyes in the back of my head. The pointing finger had *seemed* to be directed at me, but of course, Baldwin was mere inches away. Simple. It also explained the use of first name; Francis Baldwin was from one of the better-off families, and was normally a model pupil, of whom great things were expected. But now that the mistake had been pointed out, there was no need for me to stay, and with relief, I reached for the doorknob.

'Oh no,' said Mr Kent, taking his long, thick cane from his desk, 'If you're silly enough to come up in his place, you may as well have his punishment.' And he administered two strokes that set my finger-ends burning and throbbing before dismissing me.

Being a youngster, I didn't question the logic or the injustice at the time; such aberrations were not exactly rare, but later, I figured it out. Mr Kent was a disciplinarian; fidgeting was a punishable offence, but he didn't want to punish one of the better lads. Still, someone had to be punished, and quite by chance, there was a boy who was not better class, with the same forename immediately in front of the miscreant. So if the idiot went up to his room, that solved everything. The fidgeting would be punished, authority would be upheld and the boy from the better family would not be hurt. It was an inescapable fact of life that boys from better-off families never seemed to get the cane, while those from the poorer ones were over-familiar with the sting and burn. There was an element of the 'whipping-boy' about it all.

I suppose today, that sort of thing would have parents instructing solicitors and solicitors instructing counsel and the social people and human rights lobby would be in full cry and someone's head would have to roll and there would have to be adequate compensation and counselling for the stress and trauma and all the rest of today's politically correct bullshit. Well, it didn't hurt too much, and it certainly didn't turn me into a psycho who hated all teachers and growers of bamboo and better-off families. In fact later, a good while later I must admit, I was able to see the funny side, and to find consolation in the thought that there were, over the years, times when I no doubt deserved the cane and didn't get it. Perhaps it was delayed justice for the contemptible bluff in the catechism exam, so it balanced out. No complaints.

One day in September 1944, I was sitting reading, and my mother was making the dinner, when we became aware of hurrying footsteps that sounded familiar. We both looked up as the front door was flung open and my cousin, Florrie Heywood came in, her eyes swollen and red, and a piece of yellow paper crushed tightly in her hand. We both knew what it was even before Florrie blurted out the devastating news that her husband Joe had died of wounds received somewhere in Holland.

Poor Florrie, she was left with four children, all still at school, the oldest a little younger than me, the youngest in infant school. Her husband Joe was one of our very favourite people; a well-built man, he was nearly always smiling, and used to pick Jack up and hang him by the collar of his jacket on the big nail where my dad usually hung his overcoat. He would play-fight with us and throw us up to the ceiling, causing us to laugh in both delight and terror, and would join in snowball fights. An altogether wonderful man. He had joined the East Lancs in 1939, and when he was killed, had risen to the rank of sergeant, so he must have had an aptitude for soldiering. He had brought laughter and sunshine into our lives and we all loved him dearly. And now he was gone, buried in some military cemetery in Holland. The war Office later sent Florrie a picture of his grave; that and the miserable pittance of a war pension was how this great country demonstrated its gratitude for so many supreme sacrifices. His children got nothing.

About the same time, a couple of paragraphs appeared in the Blackburn Times that caused us great wonder. Dad had been awarded a medal, the military version of the British Empire Medal, for saving the life of one of his Home Guard charges on a grenade-throwing exercise in the Welsh mountains. We'd known nothing of this, nor of the fact that the wounds received in the incident nearly cost his life. He was ever a modest man, and no doubt intended to write to my mother about it when he was out of hospital and recovering.

We later learned that while instructing a particularly nervous young man, the pupil had held onto the grenade too long and it had hit the sandbags that lined the parapet of the throwing bay and fallen back between his feet. He had panicked and my dad, scrabbling to reach it in an attempt to throw it again, couldn't get to the grenade because of the man's 'freezing.' So dad, not a big man, hurled the pupil almost bodily into the shelter of the escape bay, and in so doing, was himself thrown off balance and left with no time to get clear. He dropped to the ground as the grenade exploded, showering him with fragments, one of which was later removed from within an inch of his spine, another going through the front of his shin and exiting at the rear, taking a big piece of muscle tissue. Carried by stretcher to where the ambulance could reach, he was taken to hospital and an emergency operation saved his life.

Once recovered, his CO granted him leave to collect my mother for the investiture by the King at Buckingham Palace. But unfortunately he was posted to another unit, and the new CO would not grant this leave. So Dad refused to attend, and thus the medal, now sadly lost, and a brief note signed by the King, came by registered post after the war.

The medal, being a personal award, carries the legend '3379839 Sgt J.W Burns, The East Lancs Regiment,' and the ribbon is magenta with a thin silver stripe in the middle.

Christmas was approaching, my last day as a schoolboy. I remembered another Christmas, not long after I started school. It must have been about 1937. One morning, we were told to get up quietly and form a line at the door that connected our classroom to that of Miss Wells. This simple instruction struck terror in a few hearts, for whenever unwelcome visitors arrived, the dentist or doctor, poor Miss Wells was always evicted while they set up their diabolical apparatus. And so, with pounding heart and churning bowel, I meekly joined the line.

But there was a rebel in the class. Whilst we had sorted ourselves out, one boy remained sitting, arms folded defiantly with a sulky scowl that probably masked terror on his face. Miss Kenyon glared at him.

'Didn't you hear me?' she demanded.

No answer but a deepening of the scowl.

'Get up this instant and take your place in the line.'

And suddenly the dam burst. In a voice that was bravely loud, but in which fear trembled, he said, 'I'm not going to be examined,' and continued to sit with his arms folded tightly and his lips compressed.

I admired his courage while I ached with dread for what was to come. We were then still in the infants' school and although the cane was not used, the strap was, and Miss Kenyon was not the soul of either patience or pity. We waited, scarcely daring to breathe for the wrath to come.

But, very much to our surprise, Miss Kenyon merely returned her attention to her book, ignoring this blatant act of defiance, and murmuring, 'Very well. If you don't want a Christmas present, stay where you are.'

Christmas present? What cruel ploy was this? We all knew who – and what – was in the next room, - didn't we? But suddenly, those few words echoed and re-echoed round the room. Could it really be so? Or was this some subtle adult trick to allay childish fears? We all watched the boy. Miss Kenyon ignored him and us. A minute passed. The boy's lips relaxed a little, as did his tightly-folded arms. His eyes swivelled to the line, to the connecting door, and then, slowly, he got up and joined us. Miss Kenyon read on, completely unconcerned, and just then the door opened and the first two children, one boy, one girl, were told to go forward into

Miss Wells' room. We rose on tiptoe to try to peer over through the windows of the partition, but they were too high. A minute or so later, the two emerged, eyes shining, and arms clutching toys. It was true then.

My feet began to itch with impatience, as slowly the line dwindled and we got nearer to the door. Then at last I was in the doorway and able to see into the room. The desks had been pushed against the walls, and at the far end stood an enormous Christmas tree, all brightly trimmed, and at its foot was a heap of toys. Not new, of course; probably donated by kindly people whose own children had become fed up with them, but to us, it was an Aladdin's cave. My eyes fell onto a tin police car, with two policemen, or at least their upper torsos, and wire wheels, and I prayed the boy in front wouldn't choose it. I waited in agony while he poked among the toys, but eventually, he emerged with something else and when I was told to go forward, I ran and picked up the car. Looking back, it was probably a Japanese toy pressed out of recycled food cans, but it had a wind-up motor that worked, and I thought it was wonderful ......

And now, as my last Christmas as a schoolboy came near, there was a shock in store for me. Over more than half a century, memory is inclined to be hazy, and things and events tend to blur here and there. Perhaps Mr Kent had retired, or perhaps he was sick, but at that time, the headmaster, whether permanent or temporary, was Mr Noblett, and he sent for me one afternoon. Again, as when selected for punishment while being innocent, I wondered what I had done. I soon found out, and it was more what I had *not* done. I knocked on Mr Noblett's door and was told to enter, and when I had closed the door and approached the desk, Mr Noblett looked at me coldly.

'Your attendance,' he said, without preamble, 'is the worst in the school, and the worst I have ever known.'

I said nothing. There was nothing I *could* say.

'Why have you missed so much education? Are you afraid of someone here?'

'No sir,' I replied, truthfully enough.

'You couldn't have been ill every time you were absent. Is it that you just don't like school?'

'I don't know sir.'

He studied some papers on his desk.

'You are due to leave at Christmas. Have you got a job to go to?'

'Not yet sir.'

'Do you realise that I have the authority to make you stay on at school for a further six months if I want to?'

My heart began to race. I had been imagining myself in overalls, carrying a lunch-box, bringing home a wage-packet, and now, to be told this. It was like a dash of cold water. I said nothing.

'Do you want to stay on until July?'

'No sir. I want to go to work.'

He gazed at me levelly for a while, then returned his attention to the papers on his desk.

'You don't appear to be stupid,' he said, 'so I can't think why you are absent so often, and I really feel you would benefit from a further six months. However, if you want to leave, you must not miss a single day between now and Christmas. If you do, I'll make you stay until July. Does that sound fair to you?'

It did. I made him a promise to keep up, and he dismissed me. And the threat of another six months frightened me so much that I even went to school when I could genuinely have pleaded sickness. Eventually the great day arrived, and when we were dismissed at four o'clock I walked out of the battered old gate a damned sight happier than I ever walked in.

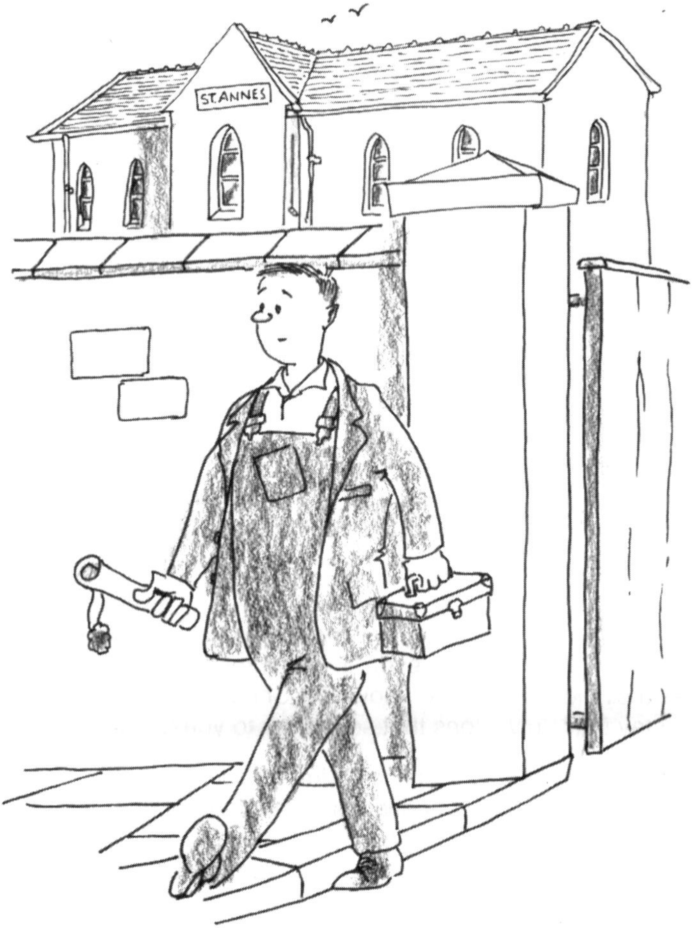
ST. ANNES

CHAPTER NINE

Work

My first job was as a warehouse lad at Scapa Dryers at Witton. We lads brought the rolls of woven canvas from the huge thirty-foot looms, set them on stands with rollers, and pulled the canvas across the surface of a long, polished table. Every five feet or so, the warp had been omitted, leaving a weak 'ladder' of just the weft. These we cut, running a huge pair of industrial scissors up the ladder and pulling the cloth over and repeating the cuts, until we had five or six lengths of canvas, which we then rolled and marked with serial numbers and piled on stillages, to await transport. I think these lengths were used to line the canisters of supplies, arms and ammunition that were dropped by parachute to front-line troops. The looms also made felts for the local paper-mills.

We worked a week 'in hand,' and that first week, when the office girl came round with the wage packets, she looked at me and asked my name and clock number.

'There won't be anything for me,' I said, 'as I only started last Thursday.' (The Christmas holiday had occurred in the first half of the week).

She rifled through the packets, paused, and handed me a packet. I was dumfounded as I checked that it bore my name and number.

'We book up Tuesday to Tuesday,' said the young woman, with a smile, 'so you have half a week.'

I looked at the slip, visible through a cellophane window. Sixteen shillings and some coppers. I'd never had so much money in my hand in my life, and what was more, I'd actually earned it. I was a proud lad when I walked in and handed it to my mother, who was as surprised as I was, and gave me half a crown spending money.

How grown up I felt that evening, as I paid for my own ticket at the King's Hall. I could also buy five cigarettes – subject to availability – since I had started to smoke at an early age. And if I wanted, I could even go to Maggie Pearson's cook-shop in Griffin Street, for a plate of potato and meat pie.

The money was good, but after a short time, the novelty wore off and boredom set in and I asked my mother if I could go to work with Jack at the Palace cinema. Jack's first love had been printing, and on leaving school at Christmas 1941, he had had an interview for an apprenticeship with a small jobbing firm on King Street, opposite the Labour Exchange. But he, like so many boys of the Depression years, was poorly dressed and the job went to a friend of the boss. Had the potential employer taken the trouble to look beyond the poor clothes, he might have noticed intelligence lurking in the keen eyes, but of course, that sort of thing only happened in fiction, and bad fiction at that. So Jack had gone to the Scapa Dryers factory but become bored with the dull routine. He tried his hand at a couple of dead-end jobs before embracing his second love, the cinema. By the time I was ready to join him, he had risen to third projectionist. There were seven projectionists, including the 'probationers,' all under the aegis of the Chief, Mr Smart. He'd been a professional footballer with Aston Villa in the twenties and had represented England on several occasions.

So when I came to ask if I could follow Jack, she let me, although my wage dropped by more than fifty per cent, from about thirty four shillings a week, to just fifteen. And for that, I had to work from ten in the morning until noon, helping with all the maintenance and cleaning that went into the job, then from about one-forty-five until whatever time the show finished, for five days a week, including Saturday. We had one day off each, Friday being traditionally the Chief's, and the lower down you were, the earlier in the week your day off. We must have been mad.

On Monday mornings, I swept and mopped, on hands and knees, the 'box,' as the projection room was known. As a rule, boxes tended to be small, often cramped, but the one at the Palace was huge by comparison, built on two levels with the rewind room, rectifier room and non-synch on the upper level, the two Ross projectors and slide projector on the lower.

The floor mopped, I next swept the stone stairs that led from Dandy Walk, twisting and turning, to the box and battery room. This room contained the banks of batteries for use in an emergency, should the mains fail, and in the annexe, there was a small veranda that overlooked Dandy Walk and the Cathedral, on which we stood to have a smoke.

The auditorium consisted of front stalls, saloon, dress circle and gallery, popularly known as the gods, or the monkey-rack, and in all, there were over two thousand seats. These, and the house lights and stage lighting arrangements, had to be maintained. Mr Smart worked to a rigid schedule, with daily tasks or chores. There was plenty to do, apart from showing films.

The Palace also had a café that served full meals, and a snack-bar overlooking the Boulevard, where patrons could get tea or coffee or minerals and cakes and biscuits. In those days, apart from the projection room staff, there were full-time cleaners, kitchen staff, box-office staff, usherettes and two doormen in long green coats with epaulets and lanyard and peaked cap and white gloves.

Then there was the manager, who wore a dress suit. There was air-conditioning, supplied by a Pleinum plant that kept the air cool in summer, and being situated on the corner of Jubilee Street and the Boulevard, it was very handy for patrons travelling by bus, tram or train. Yes, the Palace was a first-class 'town' house, and very often, especially during the Golden Age of cinema, and particularly the war years, we played to full houses, running continuously three shows a day, six days a week. The McNaghten Vaudville Circuit, that owned the Palace as well as the Savoy on Bolton Road, must have been raking in the cash, but very little of it found its way to us.

During the war, cinemas had to share a newsreel, because of the shortage of film, and we shared the Pathe Gazette with the Majestic on King William Street, opposite the old Town Hall. The

Majestic had started life as the Cotton Exchange, and had the look of a church, with arched windows, and the box was reached by means of an iron, spiral staircase. When we had run the Gazette, I would rewind it and dash across to the Majestic with the single reel (on a double spool) in a fireproof metal box lined with plywood. I really hated this chore, especially on Saturday evenings, when everyone else was dressed up and going out. I felt very self-conscious as I hurried, sometimes actually running when the time element was tight, among all these people whom I imagined were looking with either curiosity or contempt at me in my overalls, with the awkward, jangling box, whose dimensions made it impossible to carry comfortably.

High in the ceiling, directly over the stalls, was a huge cupola, or dome, and around the upcurled rim were coloured lamps, staggered in red, green and blue. Two hundred and twenty two of them, and when any of them blew, they had to be replaced. To do this, we had to mount the fixed ladder into the loft-space between ceiling and roof, and, walking very carefully, aided only by a torch beam, traverse the joists, being especially careful not to let our feet stray onto the delicate plaster of the ceiling. Having reached the dome, we had to lie face forward, on the dusty plasterboard sheeting that lay at a downward angle between the ceiling joists and the lip of the dome. In this way, we could reach the lamps, take out the duds and insert the new. This job was nerve-wracking, especially to a youngster with no head for heights, because, when in position, one could look down onto the seats in the stalls some seventy feet or so below. And for good measure, one could feel one's body sliding, slowly downwards, towards the lip and the drop. The movement was like that of a glacier, all but imperceptible, but nevertheless there. It was a tremendous relief when this particular job was completed

The house-lights were Art Deco, probably a later change to the original turn-of-the-century fittings, when the Palace had followed its original function as a live theatre. In those days, stars like Gracie Fields, Houdini, George Formby senior, known as 'The Wigan Nightingale,' and Charlie Chaplin had entertained the audiences who were quick and vociferous in their criticism. Backstage, all the old dressing-rooms, cat-walks, cables, and ropes were there, as if waiting for the return of these stars. It was very creepy back there, and was generally believed to be haunted. But by who or what, no one ever knew. It was just *creepy*.

But about these house-lights. They consisted of slim metal frames, which held small panes of different coloured glass, and every so often, these had to be taken out and washed in soapy water. Getting the glass out of those tight-fitting frames played merry hell with the fingertips and often left them raw and bleeding, but even worse was the fact that the ones in the dress circle and gallery, where the floor rose in steps, were extremely awkward to reach. The normal procedure was to employ a very tall step-ladder, and on the flat floor, this was no problem. But in the dress circle and gallery, someone had to stand and steady the ladders, which could only be mounted between the rows, as the 'legs' could not be deployed, owing to the step pattern. Mr Smart was the only one strong enough and heavy enough to support the ladders, and one of the light lads had to climb up and go through all the movements, plagued by the knowledge that should anything upset the anchor of the Chief, the ladder would probably fall forwards and precipitate him over the edge and into the saloon below.

Towards the end of the war, a rift occurred, the reason for which I cannot recall, but the outcome was that Jack and I gave in our notice.

The benign venom from the cinema bug still ran strongly in Jack's veins, and he immediately sought another berth. I, as usual, followed where he led. In this instance, he led us to an interview with the man who owned a number of enterprises, which included two cinemas, the Queen's Hall at Church, and The Ritz at Accrington. John Wilson was a self-made man, a Jack-of-all-trades and currently the Chairman of Church Urban District Council, which approximated to something like a Mayor. He was a remarkable man who could turn his hand to more or less everything from blacksmith to electrician and engineer, and had facilities for all of these trades in his extensive works on the junction of Blackburn Road and Bridge Street. We caught the tram to Church one summer evening and met him in the foyer of the Queen's Hall, where, after a short talk, he engaged both of us,

Jack to run the show at the Queen's Hall, his first Chief's job, and I to work as third projectionist at the Ritz.

Neither cinema ran matinees, so it was arranged that we both worked in the Commercial Works until tea time, which we would take in the café belonging to the Ritz, situated underneath the Howard and Bullough's Social Club on Church Street, Accrington. After tea I would report to the box at the Ritz, where there were two shows nightly, the first commencing at six, whilst Jack would go to run his show, once nightly at seven thirty, helped by one of the part-timers.

Ice-cream freezers and soda fountains were manufactured at John Wilson's workshop. Arriving at ten o'clock in the morning Jack and I would potter about quite happily, not knowing what the hell we were supposed to be doing, simply following instructions, completing the chore then asking for the next. At dinner time we usually enjoyed a meat and potato pie purchased at a little wooden cook-shop just over the canal bridge. We would then take a stroll along the canal bank before re-starting work.

At five, we would either catch the tram or walk into Accrington for tea, a set meal that never varied; a Holland's meat pie and mushy peas, bread and butter or plain tea-cake, a slice of fruit cake and pot of tea. Simple enough fare, but very tasty. And all for the staff price of sixpence.

I hadn't been long at the Ritz, when Jack managed to wangle me into the position of his full-time second, with a part-timer to help out on our respective days off. The box here was vastly different from that of the Palace, there being just room for the two old Kalee 7's and non-synch, with the cubicle-like rewind room behind and below. The equipment too, left much to be desired and the first thing we did was to carry out a comprehensive clean. Mr Smart had been a hard taskmaster, but he had inculcated in us a liking for tidiness and efficiency, and the patrons, through the medium of Mrs Osbaldeston, who cleaned and manned the one pay-box, complimented these two young newcomers on the improvement in the quality of the performances. It was very nice to be appreciated and I felt the compliments were well merited. We took immense pride in running 'perfect' (breakdown-free) shows, although how we managed this with the ancient, ill-maintained equipment and mutilated old copies of second-run films was little short of a minor miracle. If you ever saw the Peter Sellers film 'The Smallest Show on Earth,' you will be able to form a very accurate picture of the Queen's Hall.

I can't remember what Jack was paid, but my wage was twenty-five shillings a week, and after a while, we began to realise that we were being exploited, the sixpenny tea notwithstanding. Working from ten in the morning until five in the ice-cream works was nearly a full working day. And then, running the show until something like ten or ten thirty was making our working day into at least twelve hours, which was four hours longer than the normal mill or factory, where the pay was very much better, and where the extra four hours would count as overtime. We got nothing extra for either Saturday working, (this was before the Sunday cinemas), or Bank Holidays. We mulled this over and approached Mr Wilson to ask for either a rise in money or a shorter working week. At first he was indignant. What the hell, *he* had started out with a set of tools and four pounds, and by working every hour God sent, summer, winter, holidays or no, he had built himself up to where he was now. And we had the temerity to suggest we were not properly paid for what we did?

Jack pointed out that there were subtle differences. Mr Wilson had had a set of tools, which we lacked. He had also had four pounds, ditto. And he had been working for himself.

Besides, there was the nature of the work. When we spend every evening cooped up in a box, providing entertainment for other workers, there was little scope for freelancing in the industrial market. And talking of the box and entertainment, look how the 'gates' had improved since we had brought our town house expertise to his fleapit. All this was not said in so many words, but rather implied, while maintaining proper respect for our employer. After a while, he nodded and agreed we had a point.

As he hated to part with hard cash, the upshot was that from that day on, we could skip the mornings and the work in the ice-cream factory and go straight to the Queen's Hall in the afternoon. Although this didn't sound like much of a concession, it did mean that we wouldn't need to buy dinner, which would save a little, and the staff tea would remain, so after a short discussion, we agreed these terms.

On Monday and Thursday afternoons, we made up the programme, running the single reels of film onto a double spool and splicing them in the middle, to make a reel running time of about twenty minutes. There was little else to do in the afternoons, until we discovered, while changing blown lamps in the footlights, that the stage housed a grand piano, a leftover from the silent days. Jack had always wanted to play a piano, or at least to try.

And so, in our free time, we went down onto the stage and tinkled on the ivories, picking out tunes with one finger and making clumsy attempts to vamp, although everything had to be learned by trial and error.

The short flight of wooden steps that led to the stage was concealed behind papier-mâché 'walls' that had been stencilled with climbing plants - wisteria or something - and into which doors had been cut. Once through the door, the steps up to the stage and the proper door that led backstage were accessible. After a while we noticed that the door that led backstage would open with a loud *CLICK*, but we put this down to the draughts that swept about in old buildings. Still, there was something a little unnerving in these sudden openings, more so as the cinema was dark and empty, the heavy silence broken only by the odd soft sigh or thud from some unknown source. These we could tolerate, but the door was something else, especially as it was *behind* us. Still, with two of us, it was all right.

Then came a day when I felt a bit ropey, and Jack, greatly solicitous, suggested it would be best if I went home.

'What about the show?' Well, he'd manage, with a part-timer. He saw me off with indecent haste and hurried back to the piano. Without my interrupting for my periods of practice, he was looking forward to a couple of pleasant hours. He hurried through the darkened auditorium, through the papier-mâché door and up the steps onto the stage and began to play. By this time, he had upgraded from the National Anthem and Chopsticks and was attacking pieces like 'The Blue Danube,' which required the utmost concentration......

CLICK. The door behind him jerked open, causing him to hit the wrong keys. He got up and went down the short flight of steps to the door. He was sure it had been shut properly when he began to play, and it was certainly shut tight now, for he pushed and pulled and the solid ball-catch held it fast. Must have been a very strong gust of backstage draught to cause it to fly open and bang shut again, he thought, as he resumed his playing.

Minutes later the door opened again, and this time he felt a cold draught on the back of his neck. He went back to the door, which now was ajar, with a cold draught blowing through. Behind, all was in pitch darkness. The backstage light-switch was at the top of a flight of gloomy stairs, and there was no way he was going up there. Again he pulled the door to and tested the firmness of the ball-catch that held the door fast, and to prevent any further interruption he wedged it with a piece of conduit. Satisfied, he resumed his practice, but no sooner had he played a few notes when the conduit clanged to the floor and the door again opened, and now the hairs on the nape of his neck were stiff with a nameless dread. He rose and picked up the chair by two of its legs and went down the steps and past the gaping door, through the papier-mâché door. Walking backwards, the chair held over his head ready to bring it down on anyone, or *anything*, he retreated up the aisle, dropping the chair only when he reached the safety of the door that led out of the auditorium and into the grey daylight of the foyer. He recounted this little item to me that night, and I laughingly suggested he had disturbed the ghost of the pianist who had long ago accompanied the silent films, for his playing did leave much to be desired. We laughed, but all the same, there was something very creepy about that little cinema, which still stands, though untenanted.

Mr and Mrs Osbaldeston lived next door to the cinema in a house that looked as though it had once been a shop, as it still had an enormous front window. To the rear of their large living room was a small kitchen, from which a door communicated with the pay-box, so that they could enter the cinema from the comfort of their own home. 'Old Jack,' as we irreverently called him - but not to his face – looked after the repairs to the seats and things, lit the secondary exit lights, at this time being gas, and did various other chores, whilst 'Our Mag,' his fond nickname for his wife, took care of the paybox and did the lighter cleaning jobs. Jack was a rather taciturn man, and at times could be downright nasty, so we treated him with caution, especially when trying to borrow a cigarette.

Cigarettes were very hard to come by, and most smokers tried to cultivate sympathetic shopkeepers, who would save them a few 'under the counter.' Our particular supplier was the lady who ran a tiny newspaper kiosk in Church Street, near the Ritz Café, and more often than not, would let us have ten Woodbines when we were on our way back to the Queen's Hall after tea.

One evening, we were out of luck, and decided we would have to approach Jack, who sometimes would lend us a couple until the Oak Tree pub next door opened, where George, the friendly landlord, would let us have some. Old Jack didn't like our asking this favour because he smoked Players, which were bigger and dearer than Woodbines, but he would usually accommodate us if we agreed to repay three Woodbines for two Players. Which was quite reasonable, of course.

Arriving at the Queen's, we went downstairs to start the generator, situated in a small room behind the stalls, and as we emerged, were startled to hear Jack walking across the balcony over our heads. Now his last chore of the day was lighting the 'exit' gas-lights, and once he had completed this, he would go through the pay-box into his home, and no power on earth would induce him to come out. And from the footsteps overhead, we knew he had just the last one to light. A lightning calculation told us that he would be back in the pay-box before we could mount the stairs to the foyer, so we ran towards the screen, where, from halfway down the centre aisle, we could turn and see him and call for him to wait.

But when we turned and looked up into the balcony it was empty.

'Come on,' said Jack, breaking into a run for the stairs, 'we might just catch him.'

The cinema was strangely built; the foyer was at street level, and from the end, a short flight of stairs led down to the stalls, which were below street level. Another short flight led to the balcony. We raced up the stairs, and just as we reached the foyer, we were relieved to see Jack coming out of the pay-box door. We dashed up to him and made our request, which he heard with his usual poker face. Whilst waiting for his decision, I asked him if he had had to return because he had forgotten his matches or something, as we had heard him crossing the balcony a short time before. He regarded me with a stony stare.

'What are you blathering about?' he demanded, 'How could you have heard me in t' balcony? I've just this minute come out, as you've seen for yoursels.'

As he was reaching for his cigarettes we didn't press the point as he could, if the mood siezed him, change his mind. But this rather shook us, because we both had heard *somebody* cross that balcony with heavy tread, and apart from Jack and me, there had been no one in the place. It gave us much food for thought. We certainly could not have been mistaken about that heavy, measured tread. Cinemas are notoriously prone to hauntings, and an empty one is vastly different from one that is filled with light and people and laughter. After the episode of the banging door, we both, like the cowardly Lion, did — we *did, did, did,* believe in spooks.

CHAPTER TEN

A Separation

In the summer of 1945, Jack had to register for military service, and although Mr Wilson made an effort to get him deferred, it was no use. In the autumn, he had the medical examination and - to my mother's surprise and consternation – was passed A2, which meant physically fit but rather underweight, and a few days after his eighteenth birthday (December 27th) he left for RAF Padgate. It was a bitterly cold day, with several inches of snow on the ground and more falling heavily as he caught the train. My mother was really upset, remembering his serious illnesses when a child, and his delicate health, although my dad, who had been demobbed in June 1945, tried to reassure her that the fresh air and exercise would do him a power of good. In the end, she realised there was nothing she could do, and accepted it. And dad turned out to be right.

Now I was alone, more or less. Somehow, work at the Queen's had lost its lustre, and my wage – which was still twenty five shillings – hardly seemed worth the effort, especially when the National Insurance contribution, tram fares and incidentals were deducted. Quite by chance, I heard that there might be a vacancy for a full-time Second just across Bank Top, at the King's Hall, so I went across, had a short interview with the Chief, Harry Evans, and was engaged on the spot. Now this was better. The King's Hall was only two minutes walk from home, so there would be neither travelling expenses nor meals to buy. And the venue itself, although a very far cry from the Palace, was a step up from the Queen's Hall.

The manager was Joe Shields, a very affable and easy-going man, who gave us as much free time as we reasonably asked for. He had a keen sense of humour and I was very happy there. We ran a matinee every Monday and Thursday, with two shows on Saturday evening. On days when we had no matinee, and provided all our maintenance was done, Joe let us do as we liked. In that summer of 1946, we stood and watched the gangs of men knocking down the air-raid shelters in the neighbourhood, and we would sometimes accompany one of the drivers in his dilapidated Fordson tipper to the playing fields at Pleasington, where the hard-core was used as landfill for the new football and cricket pitches that were being laid. Yes, all in all, life was very pleasant, and there was the odd humorous incident, such as the morning when Joe Shields arrived with a brown paper parcel and told Harry and me to follow him into the narrow yard at the rear. We had had the painters in and there were a couple of five-gallon cans (empty) in the yard.

'Get one of those cans,' ordered Joe, 'and go and put it up on top of that pile of coke.' (Beside the boiler house, at the top end of the yard).

I did this, and when I returned, Joe had unwrapped and assembled a twelve-bore shotgun, which he now loaded, aimed and fired. The noise, in that confined space was terrific and almost drowned out the sudden cry of alarm and muffled thud, from the other side of the wall. Cautiously, we peered through the gap in the gate, to see a ladder propped against the gable end of a house in Montrose Street. Near the top of the ladder, and clinging tightly, was a rather pale young man in white overalls, while at the foot lay a mortar board and a blob of mastic and a narrow trowel.

Whether he believed Joe's explanation of the boiler back-firing we didn't know. What we did know was that the blast had peppered the can and also blown out the window of the boiler-house and so we had to get the plumber to come and glaze it.

We used to get small reels of non-returnable films, such as Food Flashes, with just a couple of minutes running-time. Over the weeks and months, these little rolls piled up. One morning, Harry filled one of the empty paint cans with these bits, punched a hole in the bottom, pushed a length of film through, then lit it. We stood and watched as the orange flame disappeared into the can, and we thought the flame had died. But as Harry started forward, with a view to re-lighting it, there came a tremendous *BANG* and the can sailed high into the air, cleared the back wall and disappeared from view. A moment later came the sound of the can returning to earth, far off, among the back yards of Montrose Street. Hard on this came the sound of a bolt being angrily pulled back and a door being flung violently open, and Harry was off like a shot into the cinema, leaving me to try to explain to ' Bobby' Bennett, otherwise Sergeant Bennett of the Borough Police Force, how we had come to 'nearly kill' his cat. Happy days.

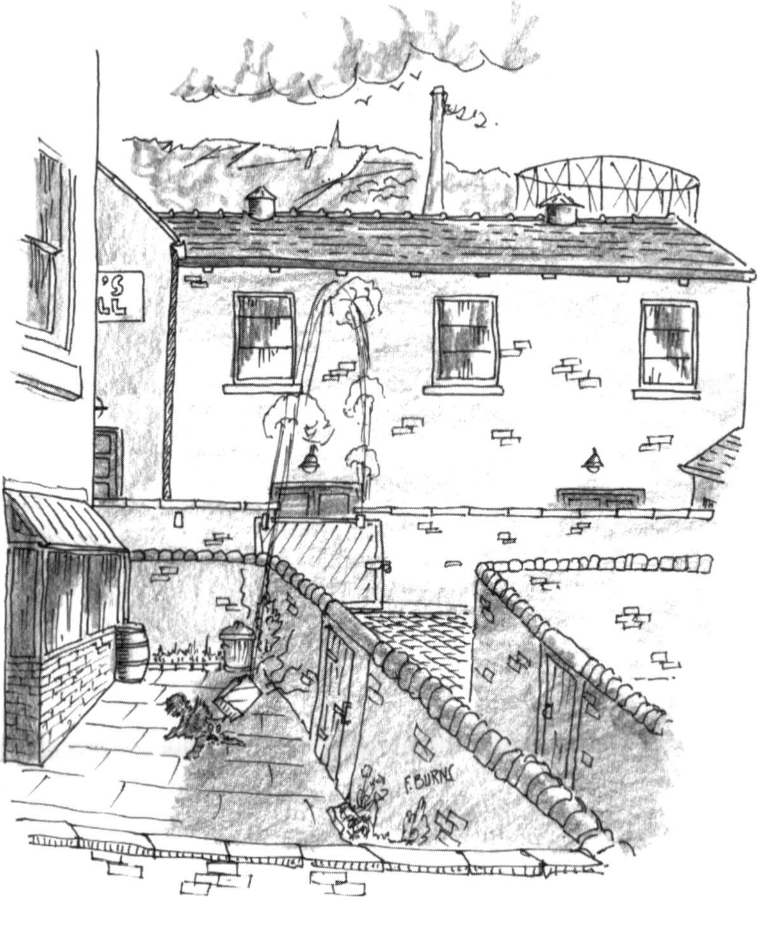
F. BURNS

On Wednesday and Saturday nights, we stripped the programme and left the cases containing the reels in the foyer, the new programme being delivered and the old one collected during the night, so that when we arrived on a make-up day, the programme was waiting for us. On odd occasions, for one reason or another, one of the films would not be delivered by the transport company, and would be sent by rail and left at the parcels office at Blackburn station where we would have to collect it ourselves. One day, I had to go and pick up a film. I think it was either an eight or ten reeler, quite heavy for a slight lad of fifteen, and those galvanised metal cases were often battered, with small jagged edges for the unwary fingers to catch. The only way to carry them was to heave the case onto your shoulder, and even then the sharp corners dug into collar bones something cruel. I was handed a threepenny piece for the bus fare – three halfpence each way – and off I went, catching the bus at Griffin, just a few yards from the King's Hall.

I crossed the Boulevard to the parcels office and collected the case. Now this was the easy part, for the case was already shoulder high on the counter. With it firmly on my narrow shoulder, I made my way to the Cherry Tree bus stop without too much difficulty. With relief I set it down to wait for the arrival of the bus. And got my three-halfpence ready. I reached into the pocket of my overalls and brought out a halfpenny, but no penny. I searched the pocket in vain, and then all the other pockets, but no penny turned up, although the bus did. I became frantic, turning out my pockets one by one, and feeling between the overalls and the trousers, but there was no sign of the penny, and the conductor was almost ready to ring off. I stepped up to him, where he stood on the platform, his hand poised over the bell-push.

'Look,' I said, 'I've just picked this film up and I've got to get it back to the King's Hall, and I seem to have lost a penny. Can I get on and I'll get the penny for you at the other end? In reply, he rang the bell and the bus pulled out.

Now what? I thought. The King's Hall was about a mile away, and this being a matinee day, and already after dinner, time was short. How long would it take me to get this film back? There was just one way to find out, and I somehow heaved the heavy case up onto my shoulder and set off, across the Boulevard and up Dandy Walk. By the time I had reached Darwen Street, a mere two hundred yards, the weight of the case was making me pant and the sharp corner was digging into my shoulder, and swapping it to the other shoulder was difficult. I was sweating as I staggered along St Peter Street, and had to rest by the church. After a minute, I heaved it up again and went on, down Freckleton Street and onto King Street, where I had to rest again. My shoulders felt like they were on fire, but then I remembered that Mr Thornber, who owned the King's Hall, also owned the Roxy, just a couple of hundred yards from where I then was, and if I could get there, surely someone would help.

I reached the Roxy, set the case down, and went up to the box, where the two projectionists listened sympathetically. When I had finished, the Second, a tall, well-built young man who was nearing military service age went with me, swept up the heavy case and set off at a fair rate, with me trotting gratefully alongside. That young man carried it to St Luke's church, the width of a street from the King's Hall, and there he transferred it to my shoulder, told me not to mention that I had had any help, and went back to his own work. He was most indignant that a slightly built lad like me had been sent for the film, and even more indignant that they had been so stingy with the money. He was certainly a friend in need, and I was very grateful. Incidentally, his father had attained some measure of local fame with his strong resemblance to Stalin, the Russian dictator. Mr Thatchell, who was very proud of his pure Anglo-Saxon name was a watch repairer and had a small shop on Bank Top.

When I arrived, I was met by both the Chief and the Manager, who were neither of them very pleased at the delay, and I explained that I had lost the penny and had to carry the film on foot. They were less than sympathetic, and Harry hurried upstairs with the case, while Joe, the manager went into his office, leaving me to get my breath. After a moment, I set off to the box, and had taken just a couple of steps, when something rolled across the floor near my foot. The penny. I can only assume that, when I thrust the change from the conductor into my pocket, it had gone between the trousers and the overalls. But why just the penny, I'll never know, as both coins had been together. And a bigger mystery was how I'd managed to walk a mile before it decided to make its appearance. There was no logical explanation. It was, perhaps, a sign of the times, that such a paltry coin could cause so much inconvenience and physical hurt. A lad today would demand a taxi, and if he lost the fare, no doubt he would have more than enough cash on his person to pay.

There was one more strange incident that I cannot explain. It was winter, and a matinee day – whether Monday or Thursday I really can't remember – and I was rewinding the last reel when Harry bobbed into the rewind room on his way down to bank up the boiler.

'Bang the mains off when you go,' he said. I replied that I would.

The mains switch was in the generator room at the rear of the stalls, and the last one out would throw the heavy switch that put out all the lights and left the cinema in complete darkness. It was easier to throw the one switch than to switch off all the individual lights. The rewinding would only take a minute or two. Or should have.

But I found several areas of damage where I had to cut and splice the film and these splices took time. As I neared the end, the lights went out. Harry must have thought that I'd forgotten, and had done it himself on his way out. He would give me a bit of a roasting when I returned in the evening, but meanwhile, there was still enough of the grey winter dusk coming through the small window to allow me to finish. The job completed, I slid the reel into its rack in the bin and set off for my tea.

Outside the rewind room was a narrow passage that ran from the top of the rear balcony stairs to the box, which was up three steps at right angles at the end of the passage. There was a door at the entrance to the passage that was kept closed by means of a counterweight on a strong cord that ran over a pulley. This door separated the working area from the rear stairs and the rear balcony doors, and ensured that the patrons would not be disturbed by any noise from the box area. It was never locked because there was no key, just the usual curved tongue that engaged in a slot.

I turned the knob and pulled. Nothing happened. I twisted again and pulled. No movement. Very strange, I thought. What can be stopping it? I peered through the now near-darkness, but could see no impediment, so again I twisted the knob and pulled and turned and pulled and …..

The door would not open. Now I was always of a nervous disposition, and I began to feel my heart beating a bit faster. I was alone in an empty cinema which was often the venue for the vehicles of Bela Lugosi and Boris Karloff and a collection of Vampires, Body-snatchers and Zombies, whose appearance and actions left indelible prints on an impressionable mind. And no amount of turning and pulling had any effect. Time was getting on, and there wasn't very much between the end of the matinee and the start of the evening show, so I decided to get a screwdriver and force the tongue free. But the box was windowless and so dark when I groped my way into it that I couldn't even see the projectors, never mind find a screwdriver, so back I went to the door, passing a now fully dark rewind room through the window of which came faint flapping sounds that I knew were pigeons that roosted in the steeple of St Luke's church, but which , in my heightened state of tension, sounded more like the leathery wings of a vampire bat, and I felt that if I didn't soon get out, Bela Lugosi would emerge from that darkened rewind room behind me, rubbing his hands and smiling that evil smile……

I turned and pulled and twisted and pulled in vain, and in desperation, I seized the cord and swung the heavy counter-weight at the lock, almost sobbing now with nervous tension. I missed the lock and split the lower panel, but still the door remained obdurately shut. I dropped the weight, stepped back a pace, raised my foot and smashed it against the lock. All I got was shock of pure agony from my ankle-bone to my knee.

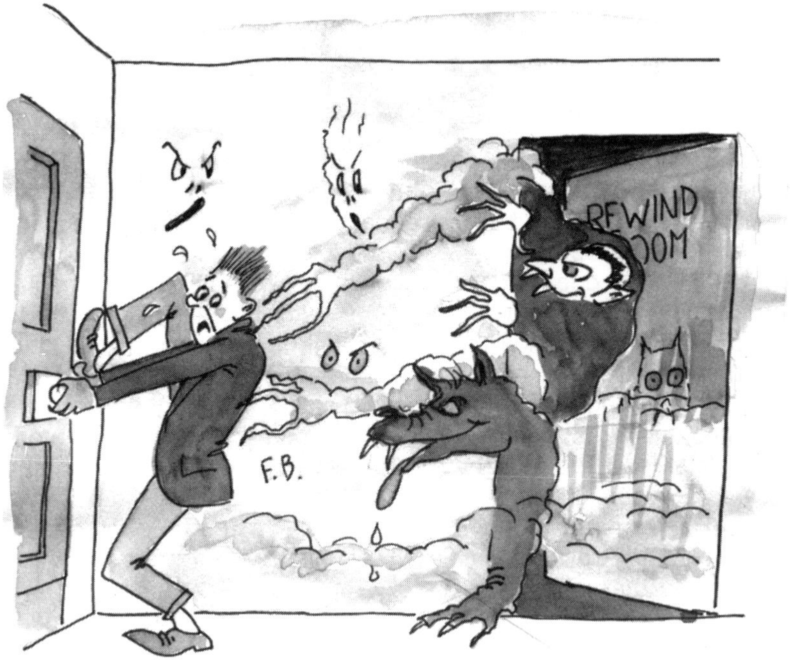
REWIND
F.B.

By now I was actually sobbing aloud, locked in an empty (?) cinema, alone; except for a legion of horrors that cackled and gibbered in my fertile imagination, and the little taps and tinkles of the cooling projectors conjured up all kind of other manifestations. With an effort of will that I hadn't known I possessed, I stood still, took a few deep breaths and told myself that I had only just left the rewind room and was going home – perfectly normally – for my tea. I turned the knob - and the door opened quite easily. For a moment, I was too stunned to move, then I was through the door and pulling open the balcony doors, fled at full tilt and in the pitch dark, through the balcony, down the front stairs and hit the bar to open the front door. I daren't think what would have happened to anyone who may have been within striking distance of those exploding doors. For a moment I drank in the sight of beautiful, normal mill-workers and factory-hands going home to tea, and I felt like Scrooge on Christmas morning. I shut the door and twisted the knob that shot bolts home, top and bottom, and it was only later, that I remembered, with an ironic grin, the name of the bar arrangement that opened the doors from the inside. Panic-bolt. Harry merely laughed when I told him what had happened, although he wasn't pleased about the broken panel, and he examined that lock very carefully, but we never discovered any reason for the incident, and to the day I left, it never stuck again. Just the one time when I was alone in the place.

Another incident that remains in my memory was much worse than being the victim of my own imagination and fears. On the back wall of the box was a 'shunt-board,' two semi-circles of copper studs with pivoting handles moving a brass contact across, to either increase or decrease the resistance to the current from the generator. One evening, with the non-synch playing and the auditorium filling, I, for some obscure reason, reached up and took hold of both of these insulated handles. Immediately I felt power surging through my body, while the sound of the record on the non-synch died away. There was a buzzing in my ears and my feet began to lift as my body was pulled upwards to the board and all the time I could feel the current coursing through my body. I thought I was going to die when, out of the corner of my eye, I could see Harry, with one foot on the base of number one projector, quite unaware of the drama behind him, watching through the porthole as the balcony filled.

By this time – which took a mere second or two – the buzzing filled not only my head but my whole being, and in desperation I shouted at the top of my lungs, although I couldn't even hear my voice. As in a dream, I saw Harry turn, very casually, and look at me with curiosity, and in that instant, I was flung from the board, the sound returned and I was left trembling uncontrollably while Harry, frowning, asked what the hell I was doing, shouting like that. He was completely unaware of the incident, and as I calmed down and told him what had happened, he more or less said he didn't believe me. But on my left forefinger was a small scar that had been a knife-cut and this was charred yellow and the skin was brittle. Don't ask me to explain what happened. I can only think that my Guardian Angel was alert and handy. We found later that one of the handles – the one I had gripped with the hand with the charred finger – had a small crack in the Bakelite insulation.

The reason I left the King's Hall was strange, and amounted to my first involvement in industrial strife. The cinema had changed hands, and the new owners were a middle-aged couple who had no experience in the trade. At the beginning, things carried on as normal - that is, our wages remained the same, as did our duties, - but the free and easy times were gone. Joe Shields had gone, because the owners were going to manage the show themselves; they didn' t like the idea of paying a manager who they considered unnecessary. This turned out to be an act of folly that had it's sequel on Easter Monday.

On Bank Holidays, we always ran two evening shows, so, with the matinee, there was precious little time to go home, have our tea and return in time to prepare for the first performance at six o'clock. Mr Beet the new owner, discussed the arrangements with Harry and at the end of the discussion, stated adamantly that he wanted the show to commence promptly at six, on the dot, 'no matter what.' Fine with us, said Harry.

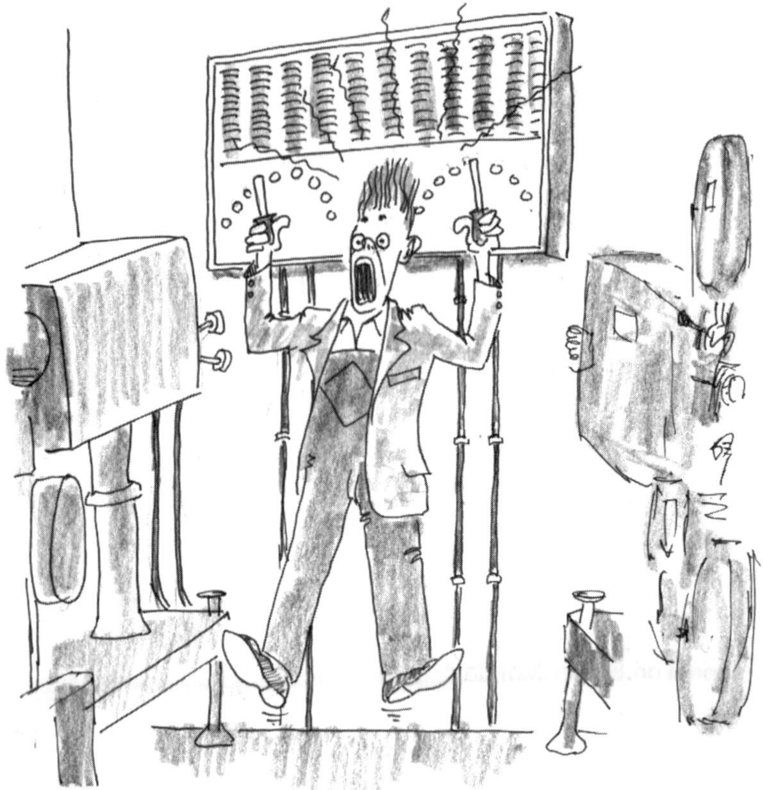

At five thirty, we were all there, ready to start. All, that is, but the owners, and as they held the only keys to the pay-box, the cashier couldn't sell any tickets. At five forty, with a queue of patrons lining up, Harry and I went to the box and started the non-synch, and at five to six, he sent me down to open the curtains (we didn't run to luxuries like electric motors, and the Second had to operate them from the backstage area) and to see if they had arrived. They hadn't. Harry struck the arc of number one projector, set the carbons burning nicely and dead on six the certificate for the second feature went onto the screen.

About ten past six, one of the usherettes came up to tell us that the patrons were still queuing at the closed paybox, and that the owners had not arrived.

'Not my problem,' said Harry, who, being a redhead, could be very fiery. The usherette retired, the show went on, the patrons waited.

Twenty minutes past six. The owners arrived, all of a fluster and while his wife opened the paybox, Mr Beet came to the box to see what the hell we thought we were playing at.

'Doing exactly what you told us,' said Harry, as we prepared for the first change-over.

This completed, Mr Beet waxed angry and told us that the patrons couldn't be expected to pay for a film that had already run for twenty five minutes. He demanded that we stop and re-start.

'No bloody chance,' said Harry, and went on to remind him that when we had asked for a little leeway between the end of the matinee and the start of the first evening performance, he (Mr Beet) had insisted that we open the show at six prompt, on the dot, and no matter what. This we had done faithfully, and, with our part of the deal done, Mr Beet could take it from there

An altercation ensued, but Harry stood fast, and in the end suggested that Mr Beet get hold of a relief projectionist, as he (Harry) would remain until one arrived and not a moment longer. He then asked me what I wanted to do and as I agreed with Harry, I said I would leave too. And so did the part-timer who happened

70

to be my cousin once removed, Gerard Derbyshire. Mr Beet gave in. He rang another local cinema and after about an hour, the projectionist arrived. Harry gave him a briefing and the three of us left.

As usual my mother received the news with her usual aplomb. The day after, Harry called and told me he was going to see about a job at the British Northrop Loom Company in Little Harwood. I went with him and we both got jobs. It was a complete break from cinema work and it was nice to finish at tea time, but hard to get up early, as I had become used to starting at ten. In the event, I didn't stop long at the Northrop.

CHAPTER ELEVEN

Bobbins And Bottles

I was put to work in the old part of Northrop, in the bobbin shop, under the beady eye of Mr Kenyon, an elderly man with a waxed moustache who wore celluloid collars and a long khaki coat. The bobbin shop was where the new arrivals went to await the next apprenticeship, and in the meantime, we sat with leather aprons across our knees and fed bobbins onto a machine that forced steel rings into the grooves, three to a bobbin, the splits in the rings staggered. We could get up quite a head of steam at this game, and the lads used to compete for speed, but it soon got monotonous. The lad on the machine next to mine would later become the central figure in what the media termed 'The Siege Of Brewery Street,' when he shot and killed his wife as well as the chief of the local CID, who had tried to talk him into giving up the shotgun. Another uniformed policeman, Jack Covell, was badly wounded. This was not my first contact with serious criminals. During my spell at the Open Air School I was once medically examined by Dr Clements, who was later tried for the murder of his wife.

One by one, the other lads were taken over to the new part of the factory to begin their various apprenticeships, and when a lad who had started after me was taken, I went to see Mr Kenyon, in his glass-walled office.

'I was here before him,' I said, politely enough, 'but he's gone over to the new building and I'm still here. That's not right.'

'Well,' he said, 'according to my information, you have turned fifteen, and so you're too old to start an apprenticeship.' (In those days, the term was for seven full years, fourteen to twenty one.) 'We want you to stay on here and take over from Joe when he retires.'

Joe Lomax was the mechanic who serviced and maintained the ringing machines, and his job was, if anything, more boring than mine. I told Mr Kenyon that I felt I ought to have been told this at first, instead of letting me waste three months waiting for something that they knew would not be, and I promptly handed in my notice. My mother was a long-suffering parent.

Quite by chance, I heard that there was a vacancy at the Roxy. This was owned by Harold Thornber, who later went into partnership with Ted Fairhurst, owner of the Palatine café just across King Street, to form the Fairthorn bookmaking firm. I went and got the job. I was back in the cinema again, full-time, at a rather better house than the King's Hall. In fact, the Roxy, which was originally the Regent, was a thousand seater, and for its time was not far short of the standard of the town houses, the Royal, Palace, Rialto and Majestic, and was about on a par with the Olympia and the Central across the street from each other. Here, the curtains (tabs) were operated from the box by an electric switch, and we could also dim the houselights and footlights. The one incongruity was that the projectors, (Kalee 7s if memory serves correctly) that still had the huge turntables attached to the bases, on which the first sound tracks had been recorded onto sixteen inch discs. Their operation more or less synchronised with the projector to 'marry' the sound to the film.

Working at the Roxy was better than at the King's Hall. We had the same matinee days, but no manager, Mr Thornber doing the job on a sort of 'when necessary' basis. As a youngster, my parents had taken me to the Regent, as it then was, and I still recall some of the films I saw there. *Hell's Angels,* '*Swing Time,*' '*Top Hat,*' and '*Ourselves Alone*', a drama about the IRA during The Troubles of the twenties, memorable to me for the incidental music, 'The Minstrel Boy.' I always liked a good tune.

It was at the Roxy that I had, as a boy, attended that indispensable institution the 'Penny Rush,' although by the mid-thirties, the price was two-pence. We were fed on a strong diet of Westerns, with heroes like Tom Mix, Buck Jones, Tim McCoy and Ken Maynard chasing rustlers, Indians and various villains all over the Hollywood back-lot. With us whistling the hero and booing the villain, the manager and usherettes patrolled with flashing torches and swinging stick in a vain effort to maintain order. Perhaps the word ought to be 'establish' rather than maintain, for there was never, from the moment the doors opened to the moment they finally closed, any semblance of order, and we only caught snatches of dialogue or music in the infrequent lulls.

It was considered great fun to hurl missiles, especially spectacular if one could reach the flickering projector beam, where apple stumps and orange peel glittered like silver moths before dropping onto some unwary head. Fights were common and part of the entertainment. If one broke out in the middle of the row, there was little chance of the manager being able to get to the offenders, as the stick he carried was merely a grown-up version of the school cane and hardly long enough. But there was one memorable day when all this changed.

There was a new manager, a stocky man with a Desperate Dan chin and fiery red head. Those within his area of influence treated him with respect, for he wielded a mean stick, but the fights in the middle of the long rows defeated his attempts, his progress being blocked by the ringside spectators. On one particular afternoon, there was a truly ferocious melee going on that looked like spreading. But like an Etruscan warrior on his way to meet Horatius and Co., down the side aisle swung the manager, and in his hands he flourished a lath that had obviously been part of a clothes-rack and measured something like twelve feet. It was an inch and a half wide and about quarter of an inch thick; a truly formidable weapon. And suddenly, the antagonists, hitherto immune from interference, found their heads, backs and backsides feeling the weight of this wonder-weapon. From that moment on, until he sought pastures new, the manager had little trouble at the penny rush.

He *did* have some with the evening trade, from one persistent gatecrasher who had a simple, crude, but very effective *modus operandi*. At the screen end of the cinema were two exit doors, covered with musty velvet curtains, and the miscreant had found some way of opening one of these from the outside. Perhaps he had an accomplice on the staff, who left the panic-bolt unfastened. Anyway, his ploy was to wait outside and listen for the inevitable cheer which greeted the dimming of the house-lights at the beginning of the show. The door would crash open, the curtains would part, and in would gallop the gatecrasher, to disappear among the paying customers who although mainly adult, still respected the code of honour in respect of grassing. By the time the usherette had brought the manager, it was too late. But the gatecrasher's plan had a weak point. It was inflexible. He always used the same door and he always chose Monday and Thursday evenings, when the programme changed. So one Thursday evening, a minute or two before the start of the show, the red-haired manager took up position by the curtains.

Down went the lights, up went the cheer, open flew the door and in rushed the gatecrasher. And down pounced the manager's eager hands, to grab twin fistfuls of the offender's woolly hair and half-turning, he set off at a dead run up the side aisle with the poor lad's clogs rattling like a machine-gun as he was forced to either run or part with his scalp. They disappeared through the curtains at the front entrance, where the sound of the clattering clogs ceased abruptly as the manager propelled him, with a little help from his foot, right across the broad pavement. The whole thing had lasted less than fifteen seconds and the manager enjoyed the healthy respect of even the tough adults from the neighbouring streets, while the gatecrashing was abandoned.

During the winter of 1946, Grandma Bamford died at the age of eighty-one, after a long illness. The day of the funeral a blizzard blew, the snow falling so fast and so thick that the windscreen wipers of the cars couldn't cope, and the poor gravediggers crouched in misery in the lee of a gravestone while they waited for the priest to finish the burial service. Which didn't take long. Poor Grandma had had a terribly hard life and although even then I could not lay any claim to devout religious belief, I sincerely hoped that there was a just afterlife, for if anyone deserved a place in Heaven, she did. She had not been a sentimental person, and at times could be downright 'nowty,' but we loved her, although we were still too young to appreciate all of the many sacrifices she had made for her family over the years.

The winter of 1947/8 was a particularly cruel one, but it did have one good thing. I came home from work one night to find that Jack was home on seven days leave. At that time, he was stationed at Topcliffe, a bomber station in Yorkshire, and as there was no fuel on the camp, all but the most necessary staff had been sent home. This was excellent news for both him and me and we were able to get in some snooker, of which I played very little since he had been called up.

Just before his seven days leave was up, he received a letter extending his leave for a further seven days, enclosing another ration card. His jubilation was short-lived, however, for almost immediately came a telegram, and I can still remember the wording verbatim. 'Disregard instructions received by post and return unit immediately, repeat immediately.'

He had the wit to leave the ration card with my mother, but when he got back to camp, another irony awaited him. Some Orderly Room clerk had recalled the wrong man. Being the sole occupant of the billet, and still without heating, in a forlorn effort to keep warm he piled up as many blankets as he could find, until he was in danger of being crushed to death under the weight.

It was shortly after the spring thaw that fate dealt me its usual hand. Mr Thornber sold the Roxy and the new owners (shades of the King's Hall) had no experience of running a cinema. They didn't actually do anything bad or wrong; it was just that they tended to make too many changes without thinking things through or asking for our views. By coincidence, the part timer was again my half-cousin, Gerard (Jerry) Derbyshire, who was a milk roundsman with Palatine Dairies. He told me that if I was interested, I had a good chance of getting my own round. He said that if I were put with a lorry driver (there were also thirty horse-drivers) you could easily learn to drive. I think it was this that decided me, and as usual, I gave notice before asking my parents, who, also as usual, gave their belated consent, And so, one morning in May of 1948, I walked up to the Palatine Dairy on St Clement Street, behind the St Thomas's football ground, and was taken on the spot

My interest in lorries had been ignited by my childhood rides with Hector, when Bank Top club was being built, and had been further fuelled by my uncle Tom. Tommy Bamford was my mother's elder brother and had enjoyed a great measure of national fame as a young man. A keen footballer, he had been signed by Darwen as a youth, and while playing for the Lancashire League team, had been spotted by Burnley, who signed the well-built, two-footed full back in 1909. By 1914, when Burnley reached the FA Cup final, he had made the right full back position his own, in the face of very keen competition.

The Final that year, played at the Crystal Palace ground, was the first to be played in front of the reigning sovereign, and when they won by the only goal, Tommy Bamford was one of the very first to receive his medal from the King's hand. The first world war broke out when he was at the peak of his career, and when it ended, four years later, he was thirty years old and beginning to struggle in the face of younger men. In 1920, he was transferred to Rochdale, where he ended his footballing career a few years later.

He obtained a job as a driver for a firm of coal merchants, J.W. Tomlinson, on Whalley Banks. Driving a tipper, he delivered coal to local mills and factories. Sometimes he would take me or Jack with him, sometimes both of us. We would meet him at the garage in Richard Street, and off we would go, both of us lads fascinated by the smell of petrol and oil and the trembling of the engine-cover between the seats. We watched Uncle Tom's big hands on the wheel and gear-lever and were entranced as the bed rose, sending the load of coal slithering out with a tremendous rushing sound. The trip over, he would drive slowly into the whitewashed garage, watching the wall looming nearer and nearer, while the ruby ignition light twinkled like a jewel on the dashboard. As it was usually a Saturday morning when he took us, he would climb down, help us down and hand us the two-pence each for the matinee. At the time, I was too young to understand the measure of his fame, and it was much later that I suddenly realised that the hard, callused hand that gave me my pennies had shaken the hand of the monarch. He never used two words where one would suffice, and he was never short of a quick answer. Like the time someone, half-jokingly remarked that he had never been a good player.

'No,' said Tommy without rancour, 'but I stopped a bloody lot who *thought* they were good.'

I think this was the essence of the man. No nonsense, no bullshit. He always called a spade a spade. A contemporary of the immortal Bob Crompton, he was equally proficient in either of the full back positions, and although he played hard, he played fair. He just wouldn't compromise with what he saw as non-essential fancy work. The way he saw it, the winger's job was to get the ball into the goal-mouth and *his* job was to stop him. Simple and uncomplicated, that was Tommy Bamford, two-footed, tough-tackling and fearless.

On one occasion, when he was lying on his back in the rain, struggling to mend a fault on the lorry, a young woman of questionable reputation watched from the shelter of her doorway.

'How much do they pay you for lying on your back like that?' she asked.

'Not as much as they pay thee for lyin' on thine,' said Tommy.

I spent my first day at the dairy with one of the supervisors, Miss Eddleston, who, I believe, had shares in the firm, and who was not above helping out when a roundsman was absent. The morning was rather cool, and I had arrived in shirt sleeves, not expecting to start that day. However I soon warmed up, and the morning passed very quickly. About half-past one we were finished and on the way back to the dairy to off-load the empties. I was told to report to Jack Clegg, one of the two male supervisors.

That day, I met one of the finest men I ever knew. He became almost a second father to me. He was the soul of generosity and good humour, with whom I never exchanged an angry word, virtues that were only surpassed by his patience with the cockiness and callowness of an emerging adolescent who on more than one occasion would have benefited from a clip around the ear.

George Collins lived with his wife May and son David in Whitehead Street, and he garaged his Morris ex-army lorry in the old City Dairy garage in Derwent Street, not far from St Anne's school, well within walking distance of both our homes. George's round was probably the most extensive at the dairy, starting on Park Lee Road, covering the old Longshaw estate, crossing to Ewood and Livesey and including the then smaller estate at Green Lane. Then on to Feniscowles, through Cherry Tree, down Feniscliffe and Witton and ending near West View at Redlam. And most of the houses had long paths. We covered some ground between us, but working with George was without doubt the happiest time of my working life. I enjoyed every minute.

About this time, my dad also started work as a horse roundsman at the Palatine. He had worked with horses as a youth and had a good rapport with them. There were about thirty horses at that time, and dad was given a big hunter named Boxer, although my dad always called him Bobby. He was a splendid animal and used to stick his huge head into the doorway when dad called home for his breakfast – he was lucky that the round he took over included his own neighbourhood – and my mother, after the initial terror, used to feed him apples and carrots. It was rather like the famous painting of rural life, 'One Of The Family.' The horse-drivers had to take it in turn to stay behind after the round to sweep out each loose-box, and feed and water the horses. For this, they were paid *a penny per horse*. Half-a-crown (12.5p) for cleaning, feeding and watering thirty horses after doing the daily round. It sounds almost like fiction, but there are men still living who would verify this fact of forties life, if asked.

Another extra chore was having to clean and polish all the tack and now and then I would help for a half-hour or so, but I was never a horseman and as soon as was decently possible, I would slip away, perhaps to go swimming with Jerry Darbyshire. After all, we were young and preferred pleasure to extra duty.

We worked *every* day at the Palatine, including Christmas day, except for the one week's holiday in the summer. We worked 358 days out of 365, and even I can figure out the mathematics of that. But we liked the work and were cheerful about it.

The summer of 1948 was a good one. The Morris had a canvas top, and early in June we rolled it back and it stayed back for four or five weeks, whilst my alabaster skin tones took on a faint tan. Jerry Derbyshire tanned easily and by July was the colour of copper. The job was seven days a week for a fixed wage. You chose your own starting time and could work as fast or as slow as you liked, but the round had to be finished. On bad days, when the lorry broke down and we spent hours waiting for the mechanics, we sometimes finished the round in moonlight. But more often than not we would be through by about one or half past, and if we finished more or less together Jerry and I would be in the swimming bath at Freckleton Street before two, and would stay there until tea time. Happy, happy days.

Nearly all of the lorries were ex-army, and three of them were Chevrolets, two American, built by General Motors, one long wheel-base and one short, the other built under licence in Canada, another short wheel-base. There were also Bedford thirty hundredweight's, a Bedford 'Scammell,' an American Ford V8 van, and an Austin ambulance like the one in the film 'Ice Cold In Alex'. Besides these, there were a few pre-war Bedfords and as time went on and civilian commercials were again being built, two tiny vehicles from the Jowett works, a Bradford van and a pick-up. These two tiny vehicles had the longest starting-handles, for the engines were very small, two cylinder I think, and occupied about a foot of space just in front of the scuttle. So the handle had to reach something like four feet to engage in the dog.

During that summer, I prevailed on George to let me have a go on the quiet roads of the Longshaw estate, and he sportingly agreed. There was virtually no other traffic, except for the odd farmer or small dairyman, and we never saw a policeman on the estate. So I soon mastered the pedals and gears, and in a matter of weeks was able to drive quite competently. All the lads learned in this manner, but none of the others had a tutor in the same class as George, who, during the war, had driven many types of vehicle, from staff-cars to armoured cars, all the way from France to Berlin shortly after the D-Day landings. His last job, before demob, had been personal driver to Brigadier General Harvey, who had commandeered a beautiful Mercedes-Benz sports car, and when George drove him to the docks for his return voyage to England, he made George a 'present' of it. It was to his great regret that he couldn't keep it.

Things were moving that summer; the country was slowly coming back to peacetime and some of the tight controls were being slackened. Milk was still strictly rationed, but now people were allowed to change their supplier if they wanted to. The Palatine salespeople, especially the two supervisors, Jack Clegg and Ernie Woodruff, were very active along these lines, persuading the customers of the many local farmers and dairymen, that they would get a better deal with the Palatine.

The dairy began to buy up these small rounds, and we found that quite a few of them were those of the men and women we met every day. And when these rounds were bought, they were integrated with ours, and so we had a lot of extra work, learning these new customers, especially as many of them were identified only by a name, such as 'Hillcrest, Livesey Branch Road.' Now Livesey Branch Road is about two miles long, and one can perhaps imagine our frustration in those early days, to-ing and fro-ing along this length, while time passed and customers waited and grew irate as we struggled to find these mavericks. And that was only one road.

And there was another problem. Most of the customers of these farmers and dairymen did *not* want to change, holding the belief that the Palatine milk was vastly inferior to milk from the farm. In fact, the dairy employed two or three drivers whose sole job was to collect milk every morning from farms in the locality and along the Ribble Valley. This was bottled the same day and delivered the following morning. The law said that the customers whose supplier sold his round were allowed two weeks in which to change to a new supplier, and a great percentage of our new customers took advantage of this and changed to another farmer or dairyman. Then the Palatine people would buy *that* round and it would come to us. The customer would change again, of course, and in the end, the Palatine Dairy was buying the same customers over and over, and no matter who the customer changed to, we were the people who turned up with the milk. It must have been very puzzling for those customers. In the end, of course, there were no more farmers or dairymen to change to and they stayed with us because they had no option.

The Palatine had depots at Preston, Bolton, Blackpool, Southport and Morecambe, and every day there was a 'run' to these, with a rota of drivers, and these runs were made after we finished our round. There was no extra pay for this. During the fine weather, these runs seemed to be done almost exclusively by the drivers who collected the milk from the farms, but now and then we would get a run to one of the seaside resorts and spend an hour or two breathing sea air.

As autumn arrived, my happy regime began to change. First I had to register for military service, and then I was taken away from George and put on the schools round with Harry Lofthouse. Harry was a decent enough man, and I quite liked him, but it was a wrench to leave George with whom I had struck up a real friendship.

Delivering milk to schools was easier, in a way, for instead of the odd pint or two, we would be depositing a large proportion of our load at every stop, but to balance this, the lorry was a three-ton Austin and the load was much bigger. It felt strange to be delivering milk to St Anne's and Bank Top, where I had 'sometimes' been a pupil not many years before. This was not exactly the local boy makes good sort of thing, but I did feel a strong rapport in these places, especially Bank Top.

On the morning of the fifth of January 1949, I reported to Majestic Buildings in Preston for a medical examination. It was a bitterly cold but fine day, and for the rest of the morning and part of the afternoon, I was poked, pushed, pulled and prodded from one doctor to another. Stripped, my body was examined from scalp to the soles of my feet, while doctors peered into nostrils, ears and mouth as if they were searching for concealed diamonds.

Towards tea time, I had an interview with an RAF officer; and was then handed a card that told anyone who was interested that I had been medically examined and passed A1. Since the outbreak of war in 1939, we had hardly ever been a complete family. Dad had been mobilised on the first of September, when the Germans invaded Poland, and had been demobbed in June 1945. Six months later, Jack was conscripted and he was demobbed in June 1948, and now it was my turn, just a few months later. My mother never had the benefit of all our wages together, and when one adds the dole years, people like my parents made some very real financial sacrifices without complaint.

The winter passed slowly and just as the first snowdrops were showing, I received another jolt at work. One morning I was told to go with another driver, who delivered to canteens and shops round the town centre. Bill Gregory drove the long wheelbased American Ford, and when we loaded the flat – a job he supervised without doing too much manual work – I couldn't help noticing that the cargo was unevenly distributed, with most of it on *my* side. The load consisted mostly of twelve gallon kits (churns), with some smaller kits and some crates of bottles, and the bed was about shoulder high, which made reaching down the big kits a difficult job.

As we drove out of the dairy, Bill told me that we 'shared' the deliveries, he delivering to the customers on his side, me to those on mine. This laconic statement served to confirm my suspicions that we were not to work as a team. The roundabout route he threaded through the town centre, doubling back on himself as often as not, was the only way he could make sure that about eighty per cent of the load happened to be on my side when he pulled up.

As I said before, reaching off those twelve gallon kits meant I had to stretch to my limit to reach the handles, then 'walk' the kit to the lip of the flat and, taking the weight on my chest, lower it to the pavement, being careful to keep my toes out of the way when it dropped the last foot or so. Then I had to roll the kit to where it was going and go back for the next while Bill sat and smoked.

And every so often (but not *too* often) he would lower himself from the cab, take off a small kit or a few bottles, and saunter into some small canteen or shop. One day with Bill was more than enough, and I made a mental vow that I would finish before I would go with him again. As things turned out, the government gave me a push in this direction, for when I got home, there was a buff coloured envelope waiting for me, with OHMS in heavy black.

Now it must be said that I had not endeared myself to the supervisors at the dairy, mainly because I was a tardy riser, thanks to the years of cinema work, with its ten a.m. starts and late finishes, and some mornings George had to rouse me. Perhaps my chronic lateness earned the switch from George, whose customers liked their milk early, to the schools round, where caretakers tended to open the gates around eight. I don't know, but it's feasible. Anyway, I had been instructed to report to RAF Padgate one week from the date of the summons, and when I went to work the following day, I was far from chirpy. So when Ernie Woodruff told me to go with Bill again, I flatly refused. I told him I was not prepared to pull my guts out while Bill sat and let me.

'You'll do as you're told ' said Ernie.

'I'm joining up on Monday,' I told him, 'so you can find another mug for Bill. I've finished, as of right now.'

Something like satisfaction appeared in Ernie's eyes, and the wet fag-end that was a permanent feature of his lower lip quivered.

'If you walk out, you won't get your job back when you get demobbed ' he said.

'I don't bloody well want it back. You can shove it.'

His eyes fairly gleamed at this, and he called on the nearest man to bear witness that I had walked off the job without notice. All right with me, I thought, and home I went. My parents accepted this latest demonstration of filial consideration with their built-in equanimity.

The following Monday, the first official day of spring, I boarded a train that would deposit me at Warrington, and from there caught a bus to the RAF camp. My civilian days were behind me for a while.

CHAPTER TWELVE

'You'll Be Sorryyyy'

We were roused by the Orderly Corporal, who marched smartly through the billet raising and dropping each bed-end to jar the sleeper into wakefulness, and exhorting us to get our warm feet on the cold deck, and with much muttering and cursing (this is the one and only time swearing at a superior did not merit a charge of insubordination, when the accused was not fully awake). We rose, dressed in our civvies and made our way to the ablutions, where the others - the ones who *had* read their call-up notices properly - washed and shaved. There were those who were regular shavers – in the cold water that issued from the taps marked 'hot,' accompanied by much banging and clattering of the pipes, while I wet my hankie and rubbed my still-fairly-smooth face. Then I picked up my mug and irons and marched to the cookhouse for a breakfast of lumpy porridge, lukewarm water, in which floated an emaciated kipper, two slices of bread with a small knob of margarine on top and a mugful of something they called tea.

The mess itself resembled the prison dining-hall in one of the popular gangster films, with benches to sit on and long bare tables that were littered with the detritus of earlier sittings. The place was crowded and by the time I had finally found a space, the only thing still warm was the tea, but I was hungry and left nothing but the odd herring-bone.

Then began a day of form-filling, under the catch-all title of 'Docs and Attestation,' being marched around the camp from place to place, and generally losing our collective memory of any life other than this. The huts seemed to huddle together for shelter from the incessant drizzle that necessitated the issue of ground-sheets to cover our civvies as we trudged around in the depressing rain. But there was a glimmer of relief. After tea, the little corporal into whose indifferent hands our welfare had been entrusted, informed us that there was an Adastral cinema not far away, and we were quite at liberty to visit, so long as we were back in the billet for bed-check at 2200 hours. So, along with two Manchester lads, I went to the cinema to watch – with great relish – a 1937 gangster film with Edward G. Robinson for once on the side of the angels. And on the following morning, we were kitted out.

'When you enter the hangar,' shouted the corporal, 'you'll find a pile of kit-bags by the door. Pick up the top one; there's a few things already in. Take it to the counter and make sure they give you all the things they call out. If there is something they haven't got, they will issue a deficiency chit. Make sure you get it and *keep it safe* or you'll be charged and have to pay for lost kit. Got that?'

Nobody bothered to answer, and he didn't press us, and we filed into the huge hangar, picked up a kit-bag and approached the long counter, behind which lurked a legion of smirking erks, eyeing us with a mixture of pity and contempt in about equal proportions.

As we shuffled along, items were dropped or tossed into the kit-bag, the suppliers calling out the official title of each in a variety of regional accents, from Aberdeen to Yeovil:

> Brushes, boot, two,
> Sticks, button, one,
> Housewife, one
> Vests, under, two,
> Pants, ditto, two pairs,
> Shirts, three,
> Collars, six,...'

And so on, as we trudged along that seemingly endless counter. Two pairs of boots were slung around my neck, one greatcoat, one best blue tunic, one battledress blouse and two pairs of trousers were draped over my arms which, even in spite of the daily exercise of the milk round, were beginning to ache from being held so long in the horizontal position. When we emerged on the far side, we were ordered to keep our new kit up, off the wet and muddy ground, and thus we staggered back to the billet, where we gratefully dropped the whole lot onto the floor and were allowed a moment to rest.

'Right,' said the corporal, after a minute or two, 'get stripped and put on your uniform; the best blue, that's the tunic. The man from the tailoring department is coming round to see to any alterations. Look lively.'

With much laughing and joking, we doffed our civvies and donned the blue, and sure enough, a civilian man and a youth came in and began to check us over. When he got to me, he turned me round, raised my arms and announced that the tunic was a little on the tight side. He made some marks with chalk and told me to take it off and hand it to the youth, saying that 'they' would let it out a bit, and whispering in my ear that 'they' would also 'get rid of those shitty Bakelite (old wartime stock) buttons.' In the event, they did neither, although I presume they were paid for both jobs. It was returned to me exactly as it was taken away, complete with the chalk-marks.

Next it was on with the battledress, or working blue, and after that each of us was handed a sheet of brown paper, a length of string, and a label, and we parcelled up our civvies and left them for collection and return to our homes.

When asked my collar size, on the visit to the kitting-out stores, I had added a half inch to my fourteen and a half, because I didn't want to be given tight collars. The storebasher must have added another inch or so, for when I put on the shirt, the neck gaped and, with the loose collar added, and the tie tightened as far as it would go without choking me, the wrinkles gave it the appearance of an Elizabethan ruff. I complained to the corporal, who told me to see him later, ordering all of us to look lively as we were going to be photographed for our Form1250, otherwise known as our identity card. So I faced the camera, holding the board on which was chalked my serial number 2426993 and the ruff-like collar was recorded for posterity.

I still shudder when I think of that Wednesday evening, without doubt the most deadly boring I ever spent in my life. After tea, the corporal appeared, bearing some items; one set of dies and a hammer; one set of rubber stamps, each bearing a single digit from nought to nine, and ink pad; and one set of stencils, each representing a digit from nought to nine.

With these, we were to stamp or mark every item of equipment, using the large stencils for the big items like the kit-bag and greatcoat, the smaller stamps for most of the other stuff and the dies for the hard bits such as the button-stick, irons and shoe-brushes. With thirty men in the billet, and no sort of pecking order, you can perhaps imagine the sheer frustration of waiting and being hurried by the next man, and by the time we were all finished, it was lights out. The up side was that we had received all our kit and it was now safely marked against theft. In four days' time, we would pack up our Padgate troubles in our new kit-bags and depart for pastures new.

Some of the better-off lads were complaining about the quality of their uniform; the cloth was rough; the boots rubbed, or were tight, or were slack, etc. But I had never been as well dressed in my life. For the first time I had *two* suits, a warm, weatherproof greatcoat (these were reputed to withstand heavy rain for up to 24 hours), enough underwear and shirts and collars and socks and *two* pairs of boots that were comfortable and waterproof. I was in the lap of luxury.

On Saturday evening, there was an announcement over the Tannoy. There would be a compulsory church parade for Roman Catholic personnel at 0800 hours on the Sunday. As I had had to state a religion when doing Docs and Attestation, I had opted for RC, so, always ready to honour a pledge, I duly rose, washed, shaved and, dressed in best blue and greatcoat. (I don't think the drizzle ever slackened, never mind stopped). I made my way to the designated meeting place, a hangar near the main gate.

Shades of my First Holy Communion. The hangar, apart from a tired-looking sergeant and a bleary-eyed corporal, was empty. I approached warily.

'Excuse me Sergeant,' I said, 'but I seem to have missed the church parade.'

He lowered a tired eye and regarded me solemnly for a moment, after which he yawned hugely and cast his eye around the immediate area before returning gaze and attention to me.

'Looks like you *are* the bloody church parade,' he said.

And with a last glance round we set off, *not* in a smart and soldier-like manner, the two NCOs talking of the previous evening's carousing. Once clear of the gates, and a little way down the road, the corporal stated to his superior that he had a mouth like the bottom of a pram, and must seek out a hair of the dog or die. I hoped it would be the latter. We marched a little further, then the sergeant called a halt.

'Over that footbridge (which crossed a railway line) you'll find the church. Can't miss it. Make your own way back to camp.'

I found it very hard to believe that I was the only Catholic in that huge intake (and a very poor example, at that), but perhaps I was just the only honest – or thick – one. Not a great deal of moral comfort there. Anyway, on Tuesday morning, we were moving to a place in Shropshire for recruit training. Some place named Bridgnorth.

CHAPTER THIRTEEN

Number Seven S. of R.T.

After breakfast on the Tuesday, we packed up all our worldly possessions, cast one last look around the dreary billet, where there were not even foot-lockers to keep our kit in, just the kit-bag at the head of the bed, and proceeded to the cookhouse to draw haversack rations for the journey to Shropshire. These consisted of two thick slices of bread, rather stale, with a hunk of cheese, *very* stale, between, and a pork pie of questionable content and age. We had been instructed to fill our new water-bottles, and this turned out to be the best bit of our packed lunch.

We walked - few knew how to march - through the centre of Warrington, the curious civilians already beginning to appear alien to us, and boarded the train, which, after a wait, gave a cheerful blast on the whistle and began to move. And, almost miraculously, as we left Warrington behind, the drizzle slowed, slackened and ceased, and a watery sun peeped out of the grey overcast. I took this to be a good omen.

I fell in love with Bridgnorth the instant we detrained at the old stone station and climbed aboard the waiting transport for our journey through this beautiful little town on the Severn. From the railway station in 'High Town,' we travelled over the bridge and through 'Low Town' on the far side and up the steep, winding road until we turned in through the gates, where the inevitable Spitfire and Hurricane waited to welcome us into the RAF proper. These looked much more sprightly than the two at Padgate.

When the transport stopped, we were ordered to jump down, and were met by a group of smart-looking young men in razor-creased battledress, a white webbing belt and gaiters, and a peaked cap with a white cover. These were the Drill Instructors, and under their direction, we entered the billets that made up 9 Flight's accommodation on 2 Wing. I was in 3/5 billet. Our Instructor told us to choose a bed-space, drop our kit, grab our irons and double down to the mess-hall, where the cooks were keeping something hot for us. Music to my ears.

Number Two Wing Mess had a frieze of cardboard cut-outs of Snow White and the Seven Dwarfs, obviously left over from the Christmas period. (Many years later I talked to men who had been at Bridgnorth long after I had left, and they told me the cut-outs were still there). The 'something hot' was a plate of corned-beef hash, barely warm, but very welcome all the same. Satisfied, we drifted back to the billets, where our DI awaited.

Introducing himself as Corporal Kellerman, he was a handsome man with a healthy tan and a voice permanently hoarse from his vocal exertions on the parade ground.

'Gather round.'

We gathered.

He allowed his gaze to traverse the ring of pale faces whilst we finished shuffling and coughing. Then, when he finally had our undivided attention, he gave us a little briefing.

'You are here to learn to become airmen. You are *not* airmen yet, not by a long chalk. You are 'recruits' and this is Number Seven School of Recruit Training. I am here to teach, and you are here to learn, and there are two ways of doing this: my way, and the hard way. My way is easy, so you would be well advised to take heed. Now, you play ball with me, and I'll play ball with you. But don't ever forget one very important thing. It's *my* ball.'

There was more in the same vein, some sound advice, some instructions about behaviour and what was demanded of us. Then we were fallen in and marched down to the bedding store to draw our five blankets, two cotton sheets and one pillow-case, something like a canvas sandbag to cover the round, straw-filled 'pillow.' Back in the billet, and with our bed-spaces chosen and kit stowed in the wooden foot-lockers under the bed, he demonstrated how to make a 'box' bed, and how to fold and square our blankets. The two sheets staggered between four blankets and the last blanket wrapped tightly around the squared-off bundle that would sit, during the day, on the pile of three 'biscuits,' the small square cushions that formed our mattress.

We were informed that we would not be allowed out of camp for 'about ten days,' save for two men who would be permitted to go into Bridgnorth on Saturday afternoon, to purchase some necessities that neither government nor RAF provided. These were an electric iron, (service trousers for the creasing of), several tins of floor polish and anything of a private nature. There was a levy of two shillings per man, and with thirty men in the billet, three pounds seemed quite adequate. Some, if not all of us, felt that having to pay for such items was not in the spirit of National Service, for all of this was not our idea, but that of His Majesty's government. Up until now, our total remuneration from the same had been, not counting the original King's Shilling, one pound, paid and saluted twice for, at Padgate on the previous Thursday. Our daily pay would eventually be four shillings, but in the meantime, we would be paid ten shillings on Thursday, after which pay-day would fall on every other Thursday, and it was up to us to budget for it to last two weeks. Out of this, we had to pay barrack-room damages, buy our own renovator for smartening up our webbing, - erroneously known mainly as 'Blanco,' which was a similar substance, but white, - soap, toothpaste, shaving soap, blades and personal items of comfort such as cigarettes and beer. Few of us drank.

Bridgnorth had three training wings, each with its own mess and Naafi and there was, naturally, quite a bit of rivalry. That first evening, Corporal Kellerman sat in the billet and answered our questions about the 'square-bashing' we were to undergo, and at 2200 hours, the Orderly Corporal called and we stood by our beds to answer bed-check. After enquiring if anyone wanted to report sick, he wished us good night, switched off the lights and left.

Five seconds or so later, he was back, switching on the lights and calling a cheery 'Wakey wakey, rise and shine' as he traversed the billet, warning us that he would be back in two minutes with a notebook and pencil to take the names of anyone still in the pit.

I blinked my eyes and gazed around. Heads were emerging from blankets, eyes as bleary and puzzled as mine must have been, as the corporal went out of the far door, banging it cheerfully behind him. I asked the time of McNeill in the next bed, and he said it was six thirty. I must have enjoyed the deepest, most peaceful sleep of my life, for it seemed as though I had barely closed my eyes. We struggled awake, put on trousers and socks and boots and went over to the ablutions. The pipes must have run all the way from Padgate, for they emitted the same bangs, groans, thumps, gurgles and cold water as those at the induction centre. I later discovered that this was common to all RAF camps.

We had much to learn. Firstly, how to march properly, and this, to some people, was not as easy as it looked. There always seemed to be at least one with the pedestrian arrangement of the camel, left foot and left arm together, and if one got immediately behind one of these, it could have the most disastrous effect on one's own sense of biped rhythm. Before long, everyone behind the 'camel' would be shuffling in and out of step like Laurel and Hardy in 'Bonnie Scotland' until the unwitting saboteur was removed to his rightful place in the awkward squad.

Even the comparatively simple art of stepping off had its complications, for often the instructor would command 'By the right,' and there were those who inevitably would step off on the right foot, despite having been told that one *always* stepped off on the left. 'By the right' simply meant that we were to hold our 'dressing' on the man to our right, and although this simple fact of life took time to settle, it eventually did, as did most things.

We learned to march, to left and right 'incline', left and right 'wheel', left and right 'turn', about turn, always with arms swinging to shoulder height of the man in front, and amazingly, we were soon quite proficient in this basic accomplishment. I for one began to enjoy the hours on the parade ground, marching, inclining, wheeling, turning and halting under the hoarsely shouted commands of Corporal Kellerman. And although he berated us from time to time, often with barely disguised contempt, we gradually came to realise that mostly it was a professional sham, designed to goad us into greater effort and concentration.

Spring came to Shropshire in a delightful lengthening of the days and warming of the sun. The clean country air filled our lungs and our pale skin began to take on the ruddy tan of good health and open air exercise. There were other things beside square-bashing. We had lectures on RAF law and discipline, aircraft recognition and sessions with the NCOs of the RAF Regiment. The Regiment had started as an army unit known as Airfield Defence Regiment, formed during the Battle of Britain, when the Luftwaffe was trying to knock out the fighter stations. These units manned the Oerlikon and Bofors light anti-aircraft guns and the Lewis and Bren machine guns around the perimeters. From there, it had been absorbed into the RAF, but still retained it's khaki, with RAF Regiment shoulder flashes and regular RAF caps and badges. They taught us things like fieldcraft, bayonet drill, unarmed combat and musketry.

After about three weeks, we spent a week on fatigues, an indispensable part of our training, and for these tasks, and for the sessions with the RAF Regiment, we were issued denims. These were khaki coloured battledress blouse and trousers, and were handed on from recipient to recipient, and I think the set that was issued to me had been around since they were first introduced in the thirties. They were truly execrable, the blouse and buttons, with bits of string substituted, were badly stained with oil, grass and other unidentifiables, whilst the trousers, undone along the length of the seam of the left leg, were held together at the bottom only by the gaiter. Why these nauseating things had not been burned long ago I couldn't fathom; perhaps they had been lying in wait for me.

And perhaps now is a good time to relate a little anecdote regarding these denims, which will also serve to underline my penchant for being in the wrong place at the wrong time.

We had reached the end of training with the RAF Regiment, and were told that we could now put the denims away, as we would not need them any more. I threw the detestable things into my foot locker with a sigh of relief and went to tea. Back in the billet, I lit a cigarette and went to sit beside Loughenberry who had the end bedspace. No sooner had I sat beside him than the billet door was thrown open and a corporal pointed at me and bellowed 'You! Get your denims on and report to the Squadron Office, chop-chop'.

By this time, I had lost most fear of NCOs and was indignant and angry. Hadn't we just been told we were finished with denims?

'What for?' I demanded.

He glowered. 'Never you mind what for, do it. Now.'

'But why?'

'Why? I'll tell you why, Laddie. Because you were nearest the door. Now move it.'

I looked at Loughenberry, who had suddenly become fascinated by the end of his fag, and as I went to put on the wretched denims, I thought about the evil, sniggering fate that had prompted me to go and sit on that spot at that time. I could only conclude that I must have a built-in jinx. And for the next two hours or so, I – entirely innocent of anything but sitting in the wrong place – joined some jankers wallahs in cleaning out and blackleading all of the coal-burning grates in the squadron offices.

Back now to the week of compulsory fatigues.

On the Sunday evening before this week of fatigues began, we happened to receive a visit from an old sweat from the permanent wing, who had a pal in our billet. He told us that the selection for the various duties never varied, and that the first twelve – the first twelve from the left side of the ranks, facing the NCO – were for the cookhouse. I took careful mental note of this snippet, and sure enough, when we paraded next morning, the sergeant, a straight-backed little Irishman named Wherity, told off the first four files of three to report to the cookhouse. Next came those detailed for ablution cleaning, and so on. I, of course, had made sure that I was as far from the first twelve as possible without being absent, and when he reached my end there were just four of us, and he eyed us narrowly, rubbing his chin and obviously wondering what he could find or invent for us. For a fleeting moment I thought he might whisper behind his hand for us to make ourselves scarce somewhere, out of sight, and out of mind. But then he told us to go along to the Squadron Office, where we would find an LAC by the name of Delaney, who would find us a job.

LAC Delaney was a ruddy-complexioned young man who wore his hat at promotion angle, i.e. dead centre, fore and aft, the two buttons immediately above his thick eyebrows, which met across the bridge of his nose. He did not seem overjoyed to see us, but scratched his head in perplexity.

'Jasus ' he said softly, 'what'll I findfer youse?'

'What about a nice quiet corner by the perimeter fence?' suggested McNeill.

We had, of course, forgotten the Irishman's love for the pick and spade. He set off at a slow roll, beckoning us to follow, and, reaching a small shed, he reached inside and handed out a spade, which I passed to McNeill, who passed it to Thompson, who passed it to Young, who had no-one to pass it to. He needn't have worried for we *all* got one, and were led back to the Squadron Office, which stood in the middle of a grassed area about as big as the Ewood Park pitch.

'Now *dis* lot has to be torned over' announced Delaney as we stared in dismay at the rough, weed-dotted surface, 'but not to worry. No hurry; nice an' steady lads, nice an' steady.'

And with this, he left us

Well, the year was at the spring, morning was at seven, and no doubt larks and snails were doing their bit with the wings and thorns, so we shrugged off our denim blouses, spat on our soft hands and set to work. And very pleasant it was, too, in that warm spring sunshine, thrusting the spade into the earth, having a smoke and a natter, lifting the spadeful and then taking a breather. I pictured the poor sods in the cookhouse and I smiled inwardly and blessed the old sweat whose prediction had been so accurate. By Naafi-break time, we had dug about fifty spadefuls, and when we resumed, it was more of the same. No-one bothered us and we bothered nobody, and life was very pleasant indeed, and when it was time for dinner, we were nearest the mess and first served.

After dinner we adjourned to the Naafi for cha and wad and a fag and a natter, and then it was back to our 'fatigues.' It seemed just too good to last.

It was.

If you have seen 'Mr McKay' in 'Porridge' you will have a near-perfect image of the Warrant Officer who appeared about three o'clock, grizzled of hair, straight of back and beady of eye. He carried a pace-stick under his arm and he stopped with a stamp of his foot, pivoted in a manner a little less formal than if he were on parade, and glared at our miserable display. I for one was not surprised when he spoke in an Irish brogue, I was beginning to think that *all* NCOs were Irish. With an eye-rolling like that of Robert Newton in 'Treasure Island,' he barked 'Ye'll finish that lot before tea if it means working through the night with *hurricane lamps.*'

We were too paralysed with shock to appreciate the Irishness of this and as he marched off – presumably to find someone to stand guard over us – we looked at the ninety per cent of unturned turf and groaned. Had we worked diligently, I suppose we would have been over halfway finished and our performance would not have raised the WO's ire. As it was, we set to work with feverish haste, digging until our hands blistered, and the blisters burst, and our backs, shoulders and arms ached abominably, and by tea time we were nearly half way through.

'God,' said Thompson, as we straightened our backs, 'this'll take all day tomorrow if that WO doesn't come back and make us work through the night like he threatened.'

'No it won't,' I said, as we shoved the damnable spades into the shed and tottered along to the billet to change for tea. 'I'll never forget Delaney's clock, but he'll not remember mine or yours. We all look alike in these bloody rags, and tomorrow, I for one will be in the first twelve.'

CHAPTER FOURTEEN

The Cookhouse

The twelve of us marched to the cookhouse, and as we entered the kitchen the permanent staff cooks were waiting. One of them fixed me with a baleful stare and beckoned me over. I went, and as I reached him, he crooked a finger and led me to a concrete plinth, the border painted white. Three enormous cauldrons, similar to cement mixers both in size and shape, were bolted onto it, and when one considers that they were used to make the breakfast porridge, the similarity extended to the content. I was handed a kidney-shaped block of wood.

'Clean these.'

I studied the nearest cauldron, its black, inner surface marred by a coating of greyish goo that seemed to average about a quarter inch in thickness. The cook was eyeing me as narrowly as I was eyeing the cauldron. I held up the wedge.

'Scrape them with this wedge?'

He frowned. 'Wedge?'

I flourished my new acquisition under his nose. His eyes grew mean.

'That's a brush ' he said testily.

I re-examined the wedge, and saw, on this closer inspection, that it did indeed bear what must have been the remains of bristles. They measured about an eighth of an inch. The steely eyes were still on me, challengingly. I shrugged.

'Right,' I said, 'is there any water?'

For answer, he reached up and turned the wheel-like tap of the four-inch pipe whose muzzle pointed into the cauldron. A gush of cold water issued forth.

'Any more questions?' demanded the cook. I shook my head, rolled up my sleeves and gripped the brush firmly. He sauntered away, whistling.

I'm still not sure if the water helped or hindered the cleaning process, but I persevered and slowly, at the expense of much energy and sweat, the grey gunge began to fade, and encouraged by this, I quite warmed to the task. Suddenly, there came a cry of *'FEET'* and I leapt onto the concrete plinth just in time to avoid a deluge of scalding-hot water that one of the cooks had flashed across the floor from a big stainless steel bucket, and which two fatigue wallahs began to push around with squeegees. I began to wonder at the logic of cleaning hard porridge from iron pots with cold water and throwing good clean *hot* water onto an already clean floor, and could only - and reluctantly – conclude that this was one of the many things intended to provide struggle for its own sake, to instil a sense of discipline into potentially rebellious minds.

As the morning progressed, appetising aromas began to circulate, lifting dull spirits. The cooks began to fill the huge trays with food, and some of the fatigue wallahs carried these to the hotplates at the servery. By this time, my three cauldrons were *clean*. I was tired and my finger-ends, which had done most of the removing of the crust, were sore enough to complement the palms, still blistered from the previous day's digging. But I was also faintly *proud* of my efforts. I was beginning to respond to the brainwashing that placed mindless chores high on the list of things to be esteemed. And while I was enjoying this rosy glow, my mentor returned and beckoned. He put out a hand, into which I released (not without difficulty) the now-naked 'brush.'

'Hands clean? he demanded.

I looked at his face to see if I could detect a glint of humour, but could see none. I didn't speak but showed him my tender, wrinkly-tipped fingers, and he merely nodded and again crooked a finger and led me to the servery and handed me a small ladle and pointed to a huge dish of custard, about the size of our old zinc bath-tin.

'Half a ladle per man,' he said, and walked away. He seemed to begrudge having to part with words.

To my left stood Thompson. Before him a tray of stewed prunes, and in his hand a small ladle. As we exchanged grins, the first of the clamouring mob arrived, and we set to work. Of course, our own Nine-Flight pals were given the biggest helpings, that was only human nature, but it cost me dear. The custard ran out and I went to ask for more. This raised a furore with the cooks. Apparently the 'half a ladle per man' should have been 'half a ladle per *two* men,' and as my mentor was keeping his mouth shut, I was deemed to have erred. To bring my wayward steps back to the very straight and exceeding narrow, I was removed from the custard detail and assigned to the tin-room.

The room was not *constructed* of tin, but was the place where all of the metal utensils were washed and scoured. It was a dreadful place of greasy floor, greasy sinks filled to the top with greasy water and steam that carried with it the blended odours of everything that had been cooked - and many that hadn't. Here, like a group of troglodytes, half a dozen erks dashed about, carrying in the caked, empty trays and pots and carrying out the warm, shiny scoured ones, in a seemingly endless rhythm, counterpointed by the curses of men whose feet slipped incessantly on the greasy floor.

Eventually, the clamour from the mess died down and finally ceased, no further helpings of meals or prunes or custard were doled out, and a strange quiet fell. In this lull, I sought out the corporal cook and asked if we were now free to eat our own meal. I was very hungry, as usual.

'Of course,' he said. He seemed to be surprised that I had asked.

'Where is it?' I asked, and he frowned at me, an amused expression on his kindly face.

'Haven't you put it away, in the hot-plate?'

I shook my head.

'Nobody told us to.'

And I thought of my tight-lipped mentor. Was the instruction to put our meal safe in the hot-plate one of the phrases his limited vocabulary could not project? Or was this further evidence of a vindictive little tyrant's sadism?

'Well, you'll have a better appetite for tea, won't you?' said the corporal.

All the tins, plates, and dishes were now washed and stacked. Two of us were detailed to go to the bread store, a small hut about a hundred yards away, in which were wide shelves, full of long loaves of bread, a tall pile of wooden trays and a slicing machine like an old-fashioned bacon slicer. One of us would slice the loaves, the other fill the trays and carry them down to the cookhouse, ready for the tea time rush. Here I must beg indulgence to relate again my ability to be in the wrong place at the wrong time.

At mealtimes, the queue was very deep and very long and moved exceeding slowly, with hunger mounting in direct proportion to eating-time dwindling, so that by the time one reached the servery, one was both hungry and anxious to feed before the time was up. On more than one occasion, my arrival at the servery coincided with the doling out of the last two slices of bread, and I was handed a long wooden tray and told to double up to the bread store and bring back a full tray.

With the tray balanced awkwardly on my shoulder, I doubled the hundred yards back to the mess, and as I entered, hands began to raid the tray, pirating the bread. If I moved to dodge the hands on the left, those on the right forced me back, and the zig-zag course ended at the servery where the tray was all but empty and I was cursed for my slovenliness and sent back. The 'wrong time, wrong place' gremlin was one I never shook off.

My colleague elected to take first spell on the slicer, so I dutifully filled the tray, set another ready for him, and carried the full one down to the cookhouse. On the way back, I passed a small anteroom, where two fatigue wallahs were putting orange-coloured cheese and raw onions through a mincing machine, and I helped myself to a couple of handfuls, wrapped it in some paper, and shoved it into my blouse. Back at the bread store, we piled this between two slices and scoffed them, and on my next trip, I repeated the theft and in this way we made up for our missed dinner.

On one of my trips to the cookhouse, I received some bad news. Our shift would be for twelve hours, 0800 until 2000. This intelligence had been excluded by the old sweat and filled me with dismay. This was Tuesday, and the evening was dedicated to cleaning and polishing – bull night. On bull night, we worked at our chores from the moment we returned from tea until all the jobs were done to the satisfaction of the DI. We were allowed a thirty minute Naafi break from 1900 to 1930, and of course, we – the cookhouse detail – would miss this, but not, unfortunately, the room-jobs we would be allocated. We would therefore be at it until lights out, as our comrades would have performed all of their chores before we even returned to the billet. It all seemed damned unfair and unreasonable, and a little group of four of us – the four who 'torned over' part of the Squadron Office surround – held a meeting, ever mindful of the fact that any subversive discussion by two or more people was regarded as mutiny, and it was decided that one of us would approach the corporal cook and beg an earlier finish. As I was the one who was already known to the cook, I volunteered to be spokesman, and we went in search of the corporal cook. He listened carefully as I pleaded our case and then nodded.

'Okay. Tell you what I'll do. I'll find you a little job, and when you've finished it you can go. How's that?'

Well, that was fine, and I mentally blessed this humane man while my pals whispered 'Good old Burnsie' as we followed him into the bowels of the kitchen. Here, in a dark, damp room were two spacious, free-standing stainless steel tanks, full to the brim with potatoes that had been through the electric 'peeler,' but dotted with eyes which glared up at us. The corporal swept a charitable arm over these tanks, which looked about as big as the ones where Barnes Wallis had tested his early models of bouncing bombs.

'Dig the eyes out of these, then off you go.'

He smiled benignly and left, and in dismay we looked at the tanks and their glaring occupants, and suddenly I was no longer 'Good old Burnsie.'

'We'll be here till bloody *midnight*,' said Thompson.

'*You* might be,' I said, 'but *I* won't.' And to elucidate, I took out my knife from the breast pocket of my denims. 'I'm going to take out the eyes of the top row,' I said, and added, 'he won't go poking in there to see what's underneath.'

The penny dropped and I was 'Good old Burnsie' again, and within minutes, we had cleared the top row and a casual glance would see no eyes peering back. Then we were off, confident that as no-one knew our names, we would not be traced. But we all decided to eat our spuds very carefully on the morrow.

Contrary to expectations, bull night turned out to be quite a happy occasion. Corporal Kellerman came in and directed operations, and under his good-humoured guidance, we polished the windows with damp, then dry, newspaper until they sparkled like diamonds, while some of the lads went outside and picked up every scrap of litter from the hut surrounds. Then all the beds from one side of the billet were moved to the other side, and we threw dollops of floor polish onto the lino and rubbed it in with rags wrapped around the heads of brooms.

For buffing, we had a 'bumper,' a wooden box with a pivoting handle and with several layers of old blanket nailed to the underside of the box, into which were piled some bricks to give weight. This was dragged up and down until the lino fairly shone, but we discovered we could improve on this by taking a blanket, sitting two of the heaviest lads on it and dragging it energetically up and down. This done, we put sheets of newspaper on the finished half, shifted all the beds to this half and repeated the process on the now bare half of the floor.

We black-leaded the two stoves, whitened the concrete plinths on which they stood, and, with razor blades, scraped the handles of the two brooms that formed a 'V' before each stove. We then attended to our personal chores, rubbing polish into our best boots - which had been packed with damp newspaper and laced up tightly – with a toothbrush handle and buffing to achieve a mirror-like finish. This, of course, was not achieved overnight, but was an on-going, almost nightly ritual that occupied about an hour of every evening for the duration of our training.

Earlier, we had carried out the trestle table that stood in the middle of the billet, and scrubbed our webbing belt, gaiters and rifle-sling, and now we finished by polishing our brasses until they glittered. And all the while we were working, there was youthful horseplay that Corporal Kellerman kept under control, while someone played Crosby and Sinatra and Glenn Miller records on a portable gramophone. Those days at Bridgnorth are at the very top of my list of fond memories; thirty strangers brought together from widely-separated areas, living on four bob a day – except for some of the better-off ones, who were sent money from home – and enjoying friendship and camaraderie quite unknown among today's young men. And the thing that struck me, as we grew familiar with each other's accents and manners, was that the poorer the area, the better were the men, with Geordies the absolute top. They were the salt of the earth, and a man who had a Geordie for a pal was fortunate indeed.

Came the day we were allowed out of camp, and off we went in the camp bus, a thirty-nine seater Bedford that carried nearly double the load on occasion. There is no better time to see

Bridgnorth than in the late spring, when the rains have raised the level of the Severn and everything is fresh and green and the air is balmy with blossom. We rode the funicular railway up the steep cliff face to High Town and roamed the streets, admiring the mediaeval town hall on its ancient arches. Straddling the main street, and all of the little town's picturesque attractions; the old town walls, with the plaque that tells of the hardships endured during the Civil War, the cave dwellings which were occupied until 1856, and the narrow winding Cartway, with Bishop Percy's House. That first visit, which was on Saturday afternoon, I lay on the lawn of and sketched the curious, leaning Castle keep. The time flew until it was time to return to camp for tea. I had never seen a town like Bridgnorth, knowing only the industrial towns of Lancashire, and I found it hard to believe that people could actually live in such beautiful places.

After the week of fatigues, we made rapid progress. We drew rifles; the Lee Enfield Mk 4, the first rifle to be mass-produced for the British forces, and rather different than the one Dad and Jack had used. We drilled with them, cleaned and oiled them and finally fired them on the fifty yard range where a concrete slab bore witness that this range had been built by NCOs of the RAF Regiment. We were lucky to have this; most recruits had to be transported to butts, which sometimes meant making a day of it, with the inevitable haversack rations.

We were due a 48-hour pass in the middle of training, but 'grants' had been introduced to coincide with Bank Holidays, and as Easter fell right in the middle of our training, we got this five days grant instead. Two days before we were due to leave, Sergeant Wherity paid our billet a visit, and his all-seeing eye fell on my best blue tunic where it hung on its wire hanger on the wall at the head of my bed. The eye narrowed, the back stiffened.

'Get those buttons changed,' he barked. 'Go down to the tailor's shop and get some brass buttons, or you won't be going on grant.'

I always seemed to be odd man out. Of the full flight of around a hundred men, I was the only one with these black buttons and the threat of being kept behind while everyone else went home put the wind up me. After dinner, down I went to the tailor's shop, where civilian women worked at long tables. I placed the offending tunic on the table before the nearest woman.

'I've got to have brass buttons in exchange for these,' I explained.

She nodded, then smiled.

'How many?'

I did a rapid mental calculation. There were four large front buttons, one small one on each breast pocket, and two on the cap that went with the best blue. In addition, one of my cap badges was black.

'Eight,' I said. 'Four large, four small, and one cap badge.'

'Right,' she said, opening a drawer 'they are three-pence each, and the badge will be ....'

'Hang on,' I said, 'Why should I have to pay? Everyone else has already got brass, free of charge. I didn't ask for these.'

'Sorry,' she said, 'but that's the rule. Do you want them or not?'

'Not.'

I swept the tunic from the table and stormed out. Sod it, I thought; I'll risk it. I really couldn't imagine that they would keep one man back for this, but to be on the safe side, when we waited for the transport, I held my greatcoat high up against my chest, covering the buttons, and I was wearing my 'best blue' cap, which had a brass badge and buttons. But still my heart was pounding painfully every time an NCO passed, but eventually I boarded the coach that would drop me at Preston.

I was the odd man out with this, too. When we went to buy our tickets from the enterprising young shark who booked the coaches, I was told that there was no one else going to Blackburn, and the nearest I could get was Preston. The fare cost me twenty one and sixpence, or a week's pay plus eighteen pence, but I paid, got the ticket and left.

When we boarded the coach, there was a hitch. The coach was a forty-one seater, and apparently the shark had booked forty two, so some poor unlucky sod would have to sit on his big pack. My backside bore the marks of the buckles for hours. Odd man out again. But all of this was forgotten in the sheer joy of going home, and the first thing I did when I landed was to cut the buttons from Jack's old tunic and take his beautifully smooth cap badge. That badge, from two and a half years of polishing, looked like burnished gold, and I became the envy of the flight, and later, when I got demobbed, it was in such demand that I made those who wanted it draw lots.

The grant over, we got stuck into training with a will. To encourage the spirit of competition, the brass had introduced a Cup for the best Flight in the passing-out parades, and Sergeant Wherity had set his heart on winning it. The main reason for this desire was that our Flight Lieutenant, a ruddy-faced man named Jeffries, who resembled Charles Laughton, had made favourites of another (previous) Flight, which had let him down on the passing-out parade and the good sergeant was determined to have the last laugh. We were *his* favourites.

There were three training wings and each of them had a Flight passing out on the same day. One Wing at 09.00, Two Wing (us, 9 Flight) at 10.00, and Three Wing at 11.00, and now that we were nearing this big day, the instructors were rehearsing us at every chance they got.

In the first week at Bridgnorth, as the rookie Flight, we had been assembled around the parade ground to watch the passing out of the senior Flight, and had been much impressed by the smartness, drill and overall fluency of the affair. We had been told that these young men had been exactly like us two months ago, and that two months from then, we would be like them. Few of us had believed it, but now, as we neared the time, we knew that we could probably match them and even surpass them, for they had *not* won the trophy.

There was one last ordeal; the Assault Course. This was a series of tests of physical fitness and willingness to risk limb if not life on the sort of things considered necessary to everyone, even those bound for sedentary jobs. The more stupid of us watched in sullen silence as the extra-large body of men reporting sick marched off with their side–packs and sneers, and we found consolation in knowing that we were tougher (though less astute, perhaps) than these obvious malingerers.

The Regiment NCO's arranged us in small units of six men, and I was number two in the first group. The whistle sounded, and the man in front of me, our number one, a tall, gawky lad who wore his hat at promotion angle, set off at a dead run for the six-inch wide plank that rose steeply to level out at ten feet. The object was to run up the ramp, across the horizontal length (about twenty feet) and jump down into the sand and run on to the next test. It was vital to get up a fair pace to reach the top. Alas, the morning, although fine, was frosty, and number one's boots skidded near the top, and he plunged off to land awkwardly and be carried off *hors de combat* by reason of a broken ankle. I was now number one.

Up the ramp at a dead run then, and along the horizontal stretch and off, to land in the sand, as per intended. What was *not* intended was for the rifle, which was slung over the shoulder, to describe an arc and bury its muzzle deep in the sand. Woe betide the recruit, had warned Sergeant Wherity, whose rifle shows any dirt when inspected at the end of the course. The damp sand must have reached several inches into the barrel and as I ran from one test to the next, I tried to dislodge it by shaking, thumping and poking, but to no avail.

On and on; climbing tall walls, swinging over pools of water, crawling under rolls of barbed wire, sticking the bayonet into dummies, screaming as we ran, and all manner of things designed to exhaust and frustrate you, while the NCOs jeered and encouraged and threatened from the sidelines. Damned good fun.

By the end of May, we were the senior Flight, scornful of the pale faces of the newer arrivals, while they were in awe of us. The few men who may have posed a problem had been weeded out and assigned other duties for the last few rehearsals, and, came the evening when Corporal Kellerman announced that he was satisfied with us, that there was no longer room for improvement. This was music to our ears, and we were encouraged to swagger.

A couple of days before the parade, we were instructed to send one collar each to a certain Chinese laundry, to be starched. When they came back, they were hard and shiny and were put aside to await the day. Some of us had been issued with the old 'Glengarry' hats, which always fell off on parade, and those who had them were told to find someone who had a beret and to arrange a temporary swap. Nothing was being left to chance.

Monday evening, we coated the rifle-sling, belt and bayonet frog (which we scrubbed nearly every evening for ten weeks, until nearly white and completely free of blemishes) with three layers of blue renovator and left them to dry, pressed our best blue, and packed all of our gear into our kit-bags, except for the items we would need on the morrow. Then it was down to the Naafi for our farewell sing-song. Being senior Flight, we were issued with circular yellow badges to wear beside the cap-badge, and these gave us priority in the Naafi queue, which was invariably long and slow. We took full advantage of this and after the sing-song, went quietly back to the billet.

The following morning, we rose, washed and shaved, dressed in best blue and, wearing plimsolls, went for breakfast. This over, we returned to the billet and made ready. Our best boots had been packed with damp paper, laced up tightly and polished (bulled up) every evening for nearly eight weeks, and the shine on them had to be seen to be appreciated.

There is another 'odd man out' tale regarding these. On the evening that Sergeant Wherity spotted my black buttons, the reason he had called was to warn us of the dangers of using a hot spoon to rub in the polish. This had been standard practice for years, and we all had done it, but on this particular evening, the good sergeant walked halfway down the billet and stopped. We were all dutifully standing by our beds, and as luck (?) would have it, he stopped beside mine.

'There will be no more using of a hot spoon on boots,' he announced, 'and I'll tell you for why. It burns the oil out of the leather and makes it crack.'

And with this, he turned, picked up one of my beautifully burnished boots with its glass-like finish, and taking the toe end in one hand and the heel in the other, bent the boot sharply upwards. The veneer of polish immediately flaked off, leaving a well-polished boot, but not a mirror-like one. He dropped the boot onto the floor, like some dead animal.

'From now on, you will use a toothbrush handle. And *no*, repeat *no*, brushes. Toothbrush handle and dusters only. And elbow grease. Plenty of elbow grease.'

I wasn't really surprised that out of thirty pairs of boots, he chose mine for this demonstration. The others, of course, merely carried on with the toothbrush handle and dusters, but I had to reduce the other boot to the same state as the 'demonstration model' and begin from scratch. The story of my service life.

We helped each other prepare that morning, and with Corporal Kellerman and the lads who had been found other duties, we donned webbing belt and best boots. We were not to walk anywhere in a normal fashion until after the parade. And at 09.40, we left the billet and waddled, flat-footed, to the parade ground, and lined up in open order, ready for the inspection by the top brass. The parade ground was surrounded by lesser junior flights with pale faces, and the remarks of the instructor came back as we were called to attention as the brass came onto the square.

The inspection over, we went through the standard drill, without any shouted commands, the time whispered by a man in the centre, so that it appeared to the spectators that we were doing the whole thing in complete silence and by some sort of disciplined telepathy. The crowning moment came when we advanced in 'review order,' just sixteen paces, and for this the band played a jaunty little air that perfectly matched the advance. And through our minds went the rather disrespectful words that some wag had penned:

'Stand by your beds,
Here comes the Air Vice Marshal,
He may have two rings,
But he's only got one arsehole,'

When we presented arms, the crash of palm slapping magazine raised echoes, and this was because we had all slightly loosened the magazine and dropped in a few little pebbles, which amplified the sound. Oh yes, we'd learned the old sweats' tricks.

Finally, all that was left was to march past the saluting-base in column of route, to the strains of the RAF March-Past, played by the Wing band, a fine group of semi-pro and amateur musicians. Then we were off, it was over and we went back to the billet, to collect our bedding for return to the stores and hand in our rifles. All that was left now − after an extended Naafi break − was to attend a pep-talk in the camp cinema and to hear who'd won the trophy. And I think none of us were surprised when it was awarded to us. And if there was elation as we boarded the transport that would take us into Wolverhampton to catch our various trains, there was also regret that we were parting company from thirty former strangers who were now firm friends. And from a beautiful little market town that spanned the Severn with its quaint old buildings. I for one had spent the happiest ten weeks of my life there, and I vowed that some day I would revisit. And I did.

CHAPTER FIFTEEN

Back To School

Among the snippets of lore handed on from old sweat to rookie were things like 'never volunteer for anything,' 'avoid the cookhouse,' and, the one most popular; 'if you were a joiner, the RAF would send you on a plumbing course; if an electrician you would be made into a joiner, if a fitter, the trade for you would be electrician,' and so on. The RAF, for all its faults, had some intelligent and perceptive people among the men who set the aptitude tests, and it may well have been that the joiner *should* have been a plumber, the 'leccy' a joiner and the fitter a leccy. Perhaps. All I know is that when we had been told to study the available courses on the board at Bridgnorth, and to select no less than *five*, to allow for the vagaries of supply and demand, I had plumped for MTD - Mechanical Transport Driver - at number one.

This was natural to me, as I had been driving before call-up, and to add the icing to the cake, this was a six-weeks course at one of the RAF stations along the Fylde coast, twenty odd miles from home, and this conjured up visions of hitching home every weekend.

There were three main RAF camps in that area, Kirkham, Weeton and Warton, and although I can't remember which taught which, there were courses for MTD, MTM (Mechanical Transport Mechanic), and Fitter Armourer, either on Guns or Turrets. These were my first three, the fourth, I think, was for Fitter Airframes, and, at a loss for the final, I just put Clerk GD (General Duties). *Nobody* entered the bottom choice, which was ' Gunner, RAF Regiment.'

When, on leaving Bridgnorth, the postings were issued, I found I was to report to RAF Wythal, Warwickshire, for a six-week course on Clerical General Duties. There must have been an acute shortage of clerks, I thought, after the initial shock of disappointment, for about ten of my pals were also destined for the course, which made it more palatable

RAF Wythal turned out to be a very nice camp, a few miles outside Birmingham near an area known as Maypole. There was both a pub and a cinema with this name, next door to each other. The June weather was glorious, we were in shirt-sleeve order and all ten or so Bridgnorth buddies were assigned the same Instructor, a laconic sergeant by the name of Musselwhite, with whom we formed a very easy and friendly association. He was a

111

first rate instructor, never used his authority unjustly, set us all at ease, and in general made the course a pleasure.

There was very little 'bull,' for the course left little time for that sort of thing, and the officers were shrewd enough to know this. There was much to cram into six weeks, which would consist mainly of reading, taking dictation and remembering all we learned, and to add to our skills we would have a course on touch-typing. It was a big camp, and the meals were taken in two sittings, with the newcomers on the first. Reveille was at 06.30, breakfast at seven, and the classes began at eight.

There was a form for everything you could think of in the RAF, and every form had a number and this was one of the main memory tests. As I recall over half a century later, our postings and appointments were on F1580, our Identity Card was a F1250, our conduct sheet a F120/121 and a 'fizzer' (Charge-sheet) as every ex-serviceman should know, was an F252. And so on, through scores of numbers.

We had to learn about the organisation, from the Air Ministry down, how it was organised, how it functioned, who was responsible for what and so on and so on. All these things were dictated by good-humoured Sergeant Musselwhite, and duly recorded in our exercise books. And for an hour or two every day, we put the books away and went over to the typing area, a kind of huge office, with big windows and perhaps forty tables, each with a manual typewriter and paper. Against one wall was a record player, on which the instructor put the records to whose rhythm we learned to tap the 'home keys' in the centre row, moving to the upper and lower rows as we progressed. Also as we progressed, the music became faster, although never too fast for any but the most inept to keep up with. And it was truly amazing how rapidly we progressed.

Half way through the course, we had an interim exam, after which we were granted a 48 hour pass. There was a note of caution; anyone who failed not only missed the weekend pass but was taken off the course and posted to Pool Flight, from where they would be posted as GDs, or General Duties. These were the 'labourers' of the RAF, whose duties included all the menial ones like coal-heaving and any heavy and/or dirty jobs that were deemed necessary. No one was really expected to fail, although there were one or two suspect cases, the ones who displayed little interest.

Because of the sheer volume of things to be remembered, there was much swotting, but I had never been one for this. I had passed the 'Scholarship' without it, and was arrogant enough to believe that I didn't need to swot. The weather was beautiful, around the camp was fresh countryside, and when on camp, the Naafi beckoned, with its snooker and table tennis tables.

Andre Thorpe was a nice enough lad, although he came from a very well-to-do family and had been at Harrow right up to call-up. Although he spoke with an Oxbridge accent, there was no edge on him at all. He used to warn me of the dire consequences of carelessness, and I, for my part, sneered. Who could fail a simple exam that was mainly a memory test? Secretly, I considered that Andre was well educated but rather thick; after all, education was no substitute for intelligence. I would have done well to heed his warnings. When the results were out, I had failed.

I was devastated, of course. Mainly because of the humiliation, but also because I would not only miss the 48, but would from now on be an unskilled labourer. The utter *ignominy* of it. Sergeant Musselwhite was sad rather than angry. He must have been accustomed to youthful egotism. So on the Friday afternoon, while the others discussed their plans for the weekend, I sat very quietly, pretending to read my notes, but seeing only doom and gloom.

In the middle of the afternoon I was summoned to the office of the Warrant Officer in charge of the course. Here it was; the axe, and figuratively speaking, my neck could feel the approaching blade. I knocked on his door and was told to enter. I went in, walked to his desk and stood to attention. He leaned back in his chair and studied me intently.

'You're Burns, nine nine three?'

'Yes sir.'

'Hmmm. You know you failed the exam?'

'Yes sir.'

'So you prefer to go into Pool Flight? '

'No sir, I was enjoying the course.'

'But not interested enough to study?'

There was no answer to this, so I kept quiet.

'Are you stupid, Burns?'

'I think I may be sir.'

He shook his head. 'I don't think so. I think you're simply arrogant and egotistical enough to think you can get through the course without having to work; that your innate cleverness will get you through. Is that a fair assessment, do you think?'

'Yes sir.'

He pursed his lips and studied me for a moment. 'You realise you've missed your 48 hour pass?'

'Yes sir.'

'Sergeant Musselwhite spoke rather highly of you. He thinks you should have another chance. I'm not so sure, but if I do decide to keep you on, I want something better from you for the remainder of the course. If I keep you on, will you promise me that?'

My heart was turning cartwheels of hope. The afternoon sun was suddenly brighter, the birds sang louder and more sweetly.

'Yes sir.'

He studied me carefully. It was the interview with Mr Noblett all over again.

'I'm going to give you your weekend pass and let you finish the course. But don't let me down. I want *work* from you. You owe that much to me and to Sergeant Musselwhite, not to mention yourself. Now go and get ready for the forty eight.'

'Thank you sir.'

I left his office walking on air, but inwardly vowing that I *would* pass. And I did. The pass mark was forty per cent, anyone with more than sixty per cent passed out AC1 (Aircraftman First Class), and his pay was increased by sixpence per diem. Eighty per cent, which was extremely rare, meant LAC (Leading Aircraftman) status and a whole *shilling* per diem.

I did keep my promise, and worked hard. So hard that when the results were announced, I had got my AC1. I felt I had vindicated two very decent men, and was certainly relieved that I had not failed them again. After breakfast, we paraded, our kit-bags packed, our postings were read out and we were handed travel warrants.

The odd man out jinx struck again. All the other postings seemed to be for two or three personnel, but my name was read out on its own. I was posted to RAF Kidbrooke, wherever that was, and some of the lads had a good laugh at this, for during the course, we had learned that most, if not *all,* of the forms we would make acquaintance with in our trade, were stored at the APFS (Air Publications and Forms Store), Kidbrooke.

'Looks like you'll be issuing soap coupons and copies of KRRs and ACIs (King's Rules and Regulations, and Air Council Instructions) said Mark Lewin, a Geordie and a good friend whom I would miss. We had been together since Padgate, which already seemed a long time ago.

We were dismissed, shouldered our kit-bags and walked down the road to the little railway station known as Hollywood, and there I parted from my pals and boarded the London train. It was the twenty seventh of July, nineteen forty nine and the sun was very hot. The train puffed through the countryside, taking me further from home than I had ever been in my life.

CHAPTER SIXTEEN

Number Four MT Company

I had heard my dad talk about Euston, which he used to pass through when he came on leave during the war, and as I dropped from the train, into the crowds milling on the platform, I got a rough idea of what wartime travel must have been like. For even now, four years after the war, Euston seemed to be a veritable sea of khaki, Air Force and Navy blue, with civilians scurrying everywhere. I approached a porter, who was trundling a hand-truck with some suitcases on it, and showed my warrant. Or tried to show it. He ignored it and me, and I began to trot alongside.

'Could you tell .....'

'Never 'eard of it,' he snapped. He hadn't even bothered to look or to listen. I gazed around, jostled by the throng, and finally went over to the Enquiries Office.

The young clerk inclined his sleek head to read the warrant.

'Tube to Victoria,' he announced, 'then ask again.'

I went down to the Underground and there was a row of ticket machines listing the destinations and the prices. I put my coppers in and got a ticket for Victoria, and when the train came in I managed to get aboard without mishap. A few minutes later, I got out at Victoria. Now what?

The clerk had told me to ask again, but I couldn't see any porters or an Enquiries office, so I began to ask passing strangers. Most of them didn't even bother to stop, but brushed by or pushed me out of their path, but finally a woman peered at the name on the warrant, tut-tutted and said I was at the wrong station and should go to Piccadilly. Another ticket, another tube ride. But at Piccadilly, I was directed back to Victoria. My money and patience were fast running out, but there was nothing I could do but keep trying.

By this time, it was mid-afternoon and I was tired, hungry and above all thirsty, having had nothing since breakfast. I tried again, and after a few attempts, a gentleman came over to me, and I use the term in its fullest sense. He was rather like a better-off version of my dad, and he smiled and asked if he could help. I told him I wanted to get to Kidbrooke and he asked, with an angry frown on his face, who had directed me here. To make a long tale short I just told him it was the clerk in the Enquiries at Euston.

'Servants,' he said, in disgust. 'Come with me,' he said, and led me to the ticket machines.

'The station you want is Charing Cross. 'I've just come from there, but I'll go back to show you the ropes.'

'It's all right,' I said, 'as long as I know where I'm going.' I didn't want to take up his time when he had obviously been at work all day, but he shrugged aside my comments.

'My son is in the army,' he said, as we boarded the train, 'and I would hope that someone would take the trouble to help him if he needed it.'

And with that, he accompanied my to Charing Cross, walked with me from the Underground station to the main line, and led me to a platform. There was a train standing here, with a letter 'P' (or was it 'S'?) in the destination window, and he led me to this and saw me into a carriage.

'You'll pass Tower Bridge before long,' he said, 'and when you do, start to get your things ready. Kidbrooke is the third stop after the Bridge.' He shook my hand and wished me luck and disappeared into the crowd, the first – and damn near the *only* - friendly person I encountered in London.

A nice surprise awaited me when I walked from the station to the camp. It was not the APFS, but Number 4 MT Company. The APFS was just down the road, and was mostly run by civilians. The Air Ministry policeman at the gate directed me to the guardroom and the RAF policeman on duty told me to drop my kit in the corner and report to the Orderly Room, just across the road in Headquarters.

I walked in and reported to the civilian in charge. Mr Sugg, filled in a F28, a small card with number, rank and name, religion and next of kin, and told him I was a Clerk GD.

'Pete there will be glad to hear that,' said Mr Sugg. 'You're his relief, and he can go on demob now.'

Peter Joiner was one of the last of the 'DOPE's, those called up just after the war for the 'Duration of the Present Emergency,' which was their term of engagement, and with no specific date for demob, they had to wait for replacements. (Since then, the DOPE had become National Service, and the engagement was for eighteen months; we were given the number of our demob group and a specific date. We would not be 'demobbed' but 'transferred to Class H of the Reserve,' equivalent to the infamous 'Z' men of the army).

I was therefore assigned to Orderly Room duties commencing on the morrow, but in the meantime Mr Sugg told me that the camp was going on August Grant on Friday, and asked if I had enough money to pay my fare home. I told him I had not, and he suggested that I fill in an application for a seven days privilege leave, which would entitle me to a warrant.

'The normal thing is to give seven full days notice, but as you've only just arrived, you obviously can't do that so we'll rush it through for you.'

One of the clerks was detailed to show me to a billet, and as it was near tea time, I was told to report after muster parade in the morning. And what a splendid little station Kidbrooke was. With only about two hundred bods, it was small enough to walk anywhere. Some camps were so vast that everyone had to ride bikes, with sometimes a trip of over a mile to the cookhouse.

Hut 'H' was very neat and clean, and there were several spare bed spaces. There were steel lockers, and central heating, no unsightly stoves marring the middle of the room, just the usual trestle table. I selected a bed space and stowed my gear. By the time I had finished, the men were coming in to collect their irons and I accompanied them to the mess. And I was certainly ready for a meal, and particularly a brew.

This mess was another surprise; the floor was tiled, the tables were set out with condiments and bread, and we helped ourselves to either tea of coffee from the two big urns by the servery. The food too was far above what I had become used to, and there was a general air of comfortable friendliness. I was beginning to like Kidbrooke.

Of course I was very much the new kid on the block, and had to take turns sitting-in with each of the clerks to learn just how things were done, as there were subtle differences between our theory and practice. But by and large, I found that the course had given me a very good grounding for my future duties. There was much to learn, and the clerks were moved around from time to time, so that they were conversant with each branch of their trade and never got bored with one and rusty with the others. Leave, postings, rations, promotions and reductions, signals, courts martial, duty rosters and all the minutiae that made up the day-to-day running of the RAF all had their origins in the Orderly Room. Mistakes made here could have results out of all apparent proportion to what may be thought of as merely a 'clerical error.'

Every day, from 08.00 until 22.00, one of us would be Duty Clerk, when we locked up HQ and handed in the keys. With an establishment of seven airmen (and two corporals who, of course did not have to do these duties), that meant only one day per week. In reality, the weekend man did both Saturday and Sunday, and we rotated the other days.

When acting as Duty Clerk, we performed our ordinary duties until twelve noon, then took a thirty-minute early lunch, the others taking the normal hour from 12.30 until 13.30. The same at tea time, tea from 16.30 until 17.00, when the Orderly Room officially closed, the Duty Clerk would remain, to be on hand for incoming signals or any other unplanned functions. In slack moments, we would keep abreast of the amendments to AMOs (Air Ministry

Orders). This was a deadly boring chore, when one would have to sift through several pages of amendments to errors that had only come to light after publication. It may entail finding a certain page in a particular volume, then a stated passage or paragraph, then a particular sentence, finally a word and the amendment might read 'delete comma,' or 'for 'to' read 'at" or something of that nature. It was time-consuming, but had to be done.

Just along the corridor was the telephone exchange, operated by three civilian women. On the door was a sign that warned that it was out of bounds to all personnel. Here, after locking the Orderly Room door, the Duty Clerk would leave the HQ keys when he went for his permitted visit to the Naafi at 19.30. Although it was out of bounds, we would sometimes sit on the grass behind the exchange on nice evenings, when we were all straight with the chores, and chat with the operator on duty. With all the offices in HQ locked up, the only things that could need our attention would come via the switchboard. There was never any horseplay or romance involved, just friendly talk; and in this way, many duty evenings were passed very pleasantly.

The camp was too small to have the usual 'Adastral' cinema, and instead, we had a 'Recreation Room' with the first television set I ever saw. It was a 'console' model, about the size of a cooker, and the tiny screen had a magnifying sheet in front of it, which did little to magnify the image, but made an excellent job of magnifying the distortion at the periphery. Still, the quality of the menu more than made up for that. It was on this screen that I first came under the spell of Tommy Cooper, listened to Beniamino Gigli, and watched the 1950 FA Cup Final between Liverpool and Arsenal.

That summer of 1949 was an enjoyable one for me. I had spent just three days on my new camp when we went home for the August grant, and as I had added seven days leave in order to get a travel warrant, I had twelve days at home. All in all, apart from the strange odd-man-out incidents, I had been very lucky up to now and I sincerely hoped the good luck would continue.

The MT was divided into three sections; Number One was light vehicles, such as staff cars, PUs (Personal Use) and motor cycles.

Number Two was mediums, fifteen and thirty hundredweights and Number Three was the heavies, the Bedford QLs, Leyland Matadors and PSVs, (coaches). Each of these sections had one of the Clerks GD attached, and were rotated with the Orderly Room. In addition, there was another unit on the camp, the Russian Language School, to which I was detached in the late summer of 1949.

The Chief Instructor was Flight Lieutenant Jones, a Liverpool man, and the other instructors, all civilians, included Count Lubiensky, Boris Ranevsky, a man named de Vriess and one named Tlattoff, if I remember correctly.

The course, which ran for a full year from early January to Christmas, was open to all services and all ranks, although National Servicemen who wished to take it had to sign on for a further twelve months. There were army types, ranging from private up to colour and staff sergeants, and the RAF personnel ranged from AC2 to Flight Lieutenant. There were no navy personnel. It was a very tough course, with exams every month, and I think that anyone who came bottom on three consecutive occasions was returned to his unit.

The work was interesting, but was not covered by my course at Wythal, and the Chief Instructor and I had to sort of make it up as we went along. He had an Imperial typewriter in his office next door to mine, with interchangeable keyboards, English and Russian, and he could hammer out the Russian faster than I could the English. I palled on with a couple of the students, and now and then we'd go to the Roxy at Blackheath. One evening, they were showing a re-run of an old Tom Walls film, and in one of the scenes, we spotted 'Old Boris,' as Ranevsky was affectionately known. On the following morning, I was having doubts as to whether it really was him, or simply an extra who looked like him. So when I got the chance, I asked him, and he confirmed that when, after the Revolution, he'd first landed in England, he had done many different things to earn money, and he *had* had a walk-on part in a film, but he couldn't even remember the name of it. So now my circle of acquaintances and relatives included film actors, convicted killers, and FA Cup winners.

Which leads nicely into the football season of 1949/50. I had always admired people like Frank Swift and Bert Williams, two of the top goalkeepers of the time, and had studied the way they guarded such a large area. For a quick calculation, posts eight feet high, crossbar eight yards long, gave a target area of 192 square feet, which was quite a lot of territory. I decided their main weapons of defence, apart from the generally accepted premise that anyone who played in goal was mad, were an ability to 'read' the game, anticipation, a built-in positional sense, and a keen knowledge of angles and judgement of pace. I rather fancied the challenge, and so, when the new season began, I offered my largely untried services to Paddy Fox, the Orderly Room corporal who helped pick the team. To my surprise and delight, I was welcomed almost with open arms. Goal, it seemed, was their main problem position.

At that time, the services had a lot of young professionals, and one of our drivers was Bill Toner, who had played for Glasgow Celtic, and was a very polished and strong centre half. With him as lynch-pin, we had quite a strong team and enjoyed some good games against neighbouring camps, particularly against the army team at nearby Woolwich. I soon found that keeping goal was both difficult and thankless, but I improved as time went on, and managed to hold the position, especially as the competition was all but non-existent. We enjoyed some good old tussles, winning more than we lost. After he was demobbed, Toner returned to Celtic, but must have been unhappy, for in about 1951, he was transferred to Sheffield United, and I saw him play left half at Ewood Park. He was unhappy too at Sheffield, where he could not force the excellent Joe Shaw from the pivot position, and so went to Kilmarnock. Whilst there, he was capped twice for Scotland. I always felt that he deserved more on the international scene, but of course, the professional ranks were very competitive.

My good luck didn't last. As Christmas approached, lots were drawn for the prize of staying behind on duty, and of course I won. I always suspected it was a fix, for at the time I was detached to the Russian Language School and was summoned to the Orderly Room for the draw. As all of the other clerks were Londoners and were on their own doorstep at Kidbrooke, they were either living or sleeping out, whilst I, being the sole northerner, deemed it highly suspicious, but there was no denying that my paper bore the cross. It was only later that I realised I ought to have demanded that the others show *their* papers, and would not have been surprised if *all* of them had crosses, but were discreetly not shown when mine, being first out of the hat, was revealed. Anyway, the deed was done, and when the camp emptied of all but a skeleton staff, I was one of the bones.

CHAPTER SEVENTEEN

Seconds Of Everything

Christmas morning. The billet lights were suddenly switched on and a voice with a strong Geordie accent, accompanied by a metallic banging, exhorted the two or three occupants of Hut 'H' to rise and shine. Groggily I opened each eye in turn and beheld two men in whites, bearing between them a large dixie from which issued steam and a tantalising aroma. Coffee - laced with rum!

Now this was what RAF life should be like, I thought, as I sat up and accepted the mugful, and thus refreshed and awake, rose, washed and shaved, dressed and repaired to the mess for breakfast. And with a mere handful of men to cater for, there was plenty of everything. Two eggs if we wanted them, or two rashers of bacon. But the tea and coffee were innocent of rum. Still, with the camp officially shut, we had no work to hurry to, and if nothing turned up that required my attention, I could stay in the billet if I wanted to. But most of us took the opportunity to hone our snooker skills, which were difficult to master when using a bent cue, often minus tip and 'chalked' by placing the tip against the whitewashed ceiling and twisting. This dodge didn't do much for the cueing, but it made an interesting ceiling and was possibly where the idea of 'Artexing' first saw the light of day.

At dinner time, the officers, by tradition, waited on us, and we could have seconds if we wanted them, and we *did* want them; perhaps not because we were that hungry, but just for the sheer novelty of sending the officers to and from the servery. There was a bottle of beer for each man, and small piles of cigarettes on the tables. And just for one meal we lived as if we were at the Dorchester.

When the camp re-opened, I, and the rest of the skeleton staff, went home for the New Year. I had to pay my fare this time, but by then I had had a bit of cash in credits and had drawn a few pounds. As usual, the leave flew by and now that the novelty of the high life in London had worn a little, I felt the pull of home more intensely. But as usual, once I was on the train, all was well. I don't think *anybody* left home, no matter how humble, with a light heart, and Blackburn in those days was a very different place than it is now; bustling, friendly and thriving, and, for all its greyness and dourness, it was *home*.

The winter passed, and in the spring I was recalled to the Orderly Room, one of the other clerks taking my place at the Russian Language school. Because I was a fair typist, I was set to producing the daily Station Routine Orders (SRO's) and Personnel Occurrence Reports (POR's). I was also the F793 Clerk, an F793 being a request for a vehicle, which had to be signed by the Commanding Officer, or if he was not available, the Adjutant.

The Adjutant was Flight Lieutenant F.T. Eades, a grizzled veteran who wore pilot's wings and a couple of rows of medal ribbons, including several from the 1914/18 conflict, in which he had flown fighters. It was hard for an eighteen-year-old boy to realise that I was taking dictation from someone who had been a contemporary of aces like Ball and Bishop, and who may – given a little imaginative boost – have encountered the Red Baron himself. He must have been in his sixties at the time, but still a fine figure of a man, with broad shoulders and craggy face. It was general knowledge that he had been a boxer in his day. I think he was one of the retired people who were recalled when war broke out and was still performing his duties five years after the conflict ended. He was still there when I was demobbed, and looked quite capable of staying on until he became a centenarian.

I had had a terrible fear of dentists since the incident at the school clinic. Although I had since had teeth removed by other dentists, it had always been an act of desperation rather than maintenance, never experiencing the painless dentistry claimed by some practitioners of the trade. I cleaned my teeth regularly, but one of my molars had been allowed to decay. while I hoped for some natural miracle to make it whole, which was arrant nonsense. One afternoon I felt a little stab of pain in the region of this tooth, and as the day wore on, it grew worse. Now we had neither Medical Officer nor dentist on camp, the morning sick parade being taken by a civilian doctor who arrived in his new Ford Pilot. So as the pain grew into agony, and the face swelled alarmingly, I had to put up with it. That night, I experienced the worst agony I ever knew in my life, so great that I felt as though I could smash my head against a wall. That night, needless to say, I never closed my eyes.

In the morning, having drunk a little tea in the mess, but without breakfast, I reported sick. The doctor gave me the merest examination before stating the rather obvious verdict that I was in need of a dentist. I had an abscess under the molar and so he prescribed two Codeine tablets, which worked wonderfully, and arranged a dental appointment for me at the RAF clinic in Harley Street that afternoon.

Lunch time came, a driver studied my swollen face as he stuffed food into his trouble-free mouth, eyeing me curiously over the rim of his tea mug. Eventually he spoke.

'Toothache?'

I nodded disinterestedly, trying to drink through one side of my mouth.

'Going to Harley Street?'

A nod.

'Don't let that bloody squadron leader get near you. He'll kill you.'

This sort of reassurance was not wasted on me, but I was too despondent, not to mention terrified, to offer comment, and as soon as I could, I exited, checked out at the guardroom, and set off for Harley Street.

I found the place easily enough, and walked past a few times, for the tooth was now all but painless. Isn't it always so? But in the end, I had to go in. Up I went, to the third floor of the rather dingy Victorian terrace house that bore the hallmarks of Services utilisation - workhouse green walls and frayed lino on the stairs. The waiting room was small and hot and there was a table with some 'Flight' magazines scattered on it, a handful of chairs ranged around the walls and an ancient cast-iron fireplace with an over-mantel on which stood a candlestick telephone. A young WAAF and a corporal were sitting unconcernedly, she knitting, he browsing through the magazines, and with pounding heart and fluttering stomach, I took a seat.

After a while, the phone shrilled and the WAAF, who was nearest, answered, replaced her knitting in her bag and departed. The corporal glanced at me, went back to his magazine. We waited.

When the phone rang again, the corporal, looking decidedly bored, flung down his magazine, picked up the phone, murmured briefly and went out. I was alone, suddenly obsessed by the knowledge that I could still walk, or run, down those stairs and out of the door. After all, who could stop me? But the thought of another night of agony drove this cowardly notion out of my head. It returned when the phone rang. I was told to report to surgery five!

Well, here I go, I thought. According to the cook in the mess, they would kill me in here, and I looked for the Squadron Leader who was to be the instrument of this. I was relieved to see that of the two occupants, one was a young WAAF in a white coat and the other was a young Flying Officer, whose face bore a great expression of sympathy as I sat in the chair. He bade me open my mouth and peered briefly, whistling under his breath at the extent of the swelling.

126

'I bet that's been giving you some gyp?' he said.

I could only nod, not trusting my voice to speak.

'Just go back to the waiting room for a moment, will you? And on the way, take advantage of the Royal Air Force's excellent lavatorial hygiene. I'll ring in a few minutes.'

Back I went and waited, and a few minutes later the phone rang.

'Ready for you now.'

I had heard somewhere that no dentist would take out a tooth while there was such an obvious swelling, so perhaps he would give me something to reduce this and take away the pain until - I was at this point in my wondering when I re-entered the room, and saw the stern-faced Squadron Leader. My knees almost buckled under me. I felt like the target of some ancient Nostradamus prophecy as I meekly sat in the chair. The Squadron Leader told me to open my mouth, peered, then pulled down my eyelid.

'Ever had an anaesthetic?' he asked conversationally.

'No sir.'

He raised a fine eyebrow. 'Not had your tonsils or appendix out or anything?'

'No sir.'

'Hmmm. Well I' m going to give you a whiff of gas.'

As he said this, he pulled something on wheels closer, reaching down for something that resembled the oxygen mask that aircrew wore with their helmets. He leaned forward and told me to put my hands in my pockets, which I thought rather strange, but orders is orders. I had already followed the advice of the young Flying Officer and visited their 'excellent toilet facilities,' so my bladder should present no problem, either to them or to me.

'Just breathe nice and easy,' said the Squadron Leader as he lowered the hissing mask towards my face, 'and start to count back from a hundred. With me now, ninety nine ......'

I think I got to about eighty and then, from far away came a sort of throbbing, like the drone of a German bomber. And then an echoing voice, quite faint and far off, was talking, and I could make out the words as the throbbing subsided.

'That's the ticket. Take the bowl from the nurse and rinse out your mouth.'

I saw a female hand holding a shiny bowl and I reached for it, but my hand wouldn't go where I wanted it to go. She gently took my hand and placed the bowl in it, and after a couple of dummy runs, I was able to get it to my mouth and rinse.

'We took two,' said the Flying Officer, 'to save you having to come back.'

I was very nearly normal by this time, and the nurse took away the bowl and handed me a large piece of gauze.

'Just sit still for a moment,' said the Flying Officer (there was no sign of the murderous Squadron Leader) 'and then you'll be fine.'

And I was. I couldn't believe it, but the troublesome molar – and its next-door neighbour – had been removed, and although my jaw hurt and I was bleeding, I knew that the source of the pain was gone and the relief was unimaginable. The nurse was the most beautiful girl I had ever seen and the Flying Officer was the very epitome of upper class benevolence and compassion. I smiled, thanked them both and left. What matter if I attracted curious glances on the Underground as I returned to camp? I knew I was pale and had dark rings under my eyes, and no doubt I was a little wobbly still, but my heart was light.

I arrived just before tea time, and managed to grab another mug of tea before returning to the Orderly Room to carry on with my duty turn. It would have been nice if one of the others had volunteered to swap with me, but of course, no-one did, and when they had gone I decided 'to hell with the AMO's' and settled myself down to rest. There was a tap on the door, and in came Marge, the young telephonist, bearing a glass of warm milk and two aspirins. I felt a great affection for her and was most grateful for her thoughtfulness. She was – and is – one of my happiest and brightest memories of London.

I was returning from a 48 one Monday morning (Mr Sugg always gave me an extension to cover the hours between 23.59 hours on the Sunday and muster parade at 08.00 on Monday), and I travelled on the night mail train from Preston, arriving in Euston at about 03.50 and getting back to camp at about six. Waiting at Charing Cross for the Underground to open at five, I purchased a paper. The headlines announced that War had broken out in Korea. Immediately I wondered how this would affect the National Service term. The news had caused hardly a ripple at camp, except that there was a signal instruction from the Air Ministry to the effect that as of the time of origin of the signal, all charges were to carry the words 'Whilst on active service.' So I was now on active service!

I was due for demob in September, and prepared myself for the worst. As much as I enjoyed being at Kidbrooke, I wanted to get back to Blackburn and my family. A couple of weeks later, it looked as though I would have to wait, as the National Service term was being extended to two years, a further six months, but then I read a bit further and saw that this would not include personnel whose term was up before October the first. On demob, I was entitled to eighteen days leave, but this was outside my term of engagement, which expired on September twenty first, so I missed the extra six months by nine days. Not so some of the regulars, whose transfer had to be put on the back burner.

This was sheer bad luck, but it happened, and there was nothing anyone could do about it. To illustrate the point, I'll tell about a cousin of mine, Gerard Greenwood.

He tried to join the police force, but with so many young men, they could be very choosy and one had to measure six feet in stocking feet to qualify. Gerard was five feet eleven and a bit, and he was told to go home, get a good night's sleep and return in the morning, as it was a well known fact that people were taller in the morning. This he did, and was measured at five feet eleven and three-quarter inches, and was rejected. He joined up in the regular army, for a term of seven years with the colours and five on the reserve. That was in 1938, and when his seven years were up in the summer of 1945, he went on the reserve. The Korean War started when he had still eleven days to go, and almost immediately he was recalled, serving two and a half years in Korea where he was wounded. The services could be very unfeeling.

As the days shortened, I began marking them on my calendar, and a couple of days before I was due to leave, I began to clear the camp, handing in the items of clothing and kit I would not need, but keeping some for any reserve training I might be called upon to serve. On the morning of the twenty first of September 1950, I handed in my bedding, collected my pay on a casual pay parade, said goodbye to my pals, and especially to Marge in the exchange, picked up my papers and my ticket from the guardroom and caught the train that would begin my journey back north.

I had thoroughly enjoyed the eighteen months, particularly the time at Bridgnorth and Kidbrooke, but it was nice to be going home for good, and I was looking forward to finding a job and settling down again. I didn't really fancy the tying hours and conditions of cinema work again, and I had burned my boats at the Palatine dairy, so I would be starting from scratch. But all that was for the future, but for the present the day was warm and soft, with just a hint of approaching autumn in the curling of the leaves, or as Betjeman phrased it so beautifully, 'Changeful nip of early Autumn.' I was young, healthy and my own master. What more could anyone ask?

CHAPTER EIGHTEEN

Palaces and Paper-mills

The second world war had been over for five years, and although we still had rationing – in fact, many things were in shorter supply than they had been during hostilities – we had a wonderful opportunity to make great steps forward for the people who had lived through the Great Depression and had fought and sacrificed to preserve freedom in a world that had been threatened as never before in the darkest of the Dark Ages.

People had learned much during the war, one of which being that the modern world had no room for 'ruling' and 'working' classes, at least not in the long-accepted feudal manner, with wealth and position alone determining who should rule and who should work. And with this in mind, they voted out the old rulers even though Churchill had been the undoubted saviour of the country. But they realised, as never before, that he could not have done it without them, and they wanted their say in the peace and they wanted improved lives, free of the constant threat of unemployment and exploitation. They wanted decent – not lavish – houses, with things they felt entitled to; electricity, hot water, a bathroom and a garden. These were not great demands, but under the old system, they would have been shelved now that the emergency was over and promises needn't be kept. Well, they'd fought for six long years to preserve the right to ask for these things, not cap-in-hand, and tugging forelocks, but on an equal footing with the people who had always had so much more but had – with a few honourable exceptions - given so much less. So Churchill went and in came the new hope for the masses.

I spent the greater part of my National Service in London, seeing first-hand the bombed areas, mostly cleared, ready for the re-building. What an opportunity for rebirth, for steady advancement for all.

During training – we were still taught how to advance in a bayonet-charge – one of the recruits asked the instructor at what speed a bayonet-charge advanced. And I smiled inwardly, imagining the confusion this naïve question would cause. Not a bit of it. Sergeant Locke merely nodded to acknowledge the shrewdness of the question.

'At the speed of the slowest man,' he said.

And this gem of wisdom stuck in my memory.

I had one day of leave for each month of service, but decided I would take just a week for a sort of holiday before seeking work. Jack, my older brother, had returned to the Palace, to carry on his love affair with moving pictures, and as luck would have it, was recuperating from a bout of 'flu' when I arrived home on demob, so we had a week of leisure together. He had bought a bike from a pal of his, and he urged me to buy an old bone-shaker that Bob Dawson, his future brother-in-law, had for sale. And although I had never been happy or confident on two wheels, the fine autumn weather wove its magic and I succumbed.

The bike was old and well-worn, and it had one or two interesting idiosyncrasies; the drop-head handlebars tended to drop even further, and with dramatic suddenness if one rode over a raised stone or a pothole. The saddle could never be fully tightened, and had a tendency to tip backwards as the handlebars dropped, which presented interesting and involuntary reactions. The handlebars threatened to deliver the chin onto the front mudguard, while the rising saddle crushed the scrotum, bringing tears to one's eyes. However, with the blind optimism of youth, I accompanied Jack on a ride through the playing fields of Pleasington. The weather was glorious, the autumn sun warm, and it was just good to be alive as we began the gradual descent towards the ancient Butler's Bridge.

With no gears, just a free wheel, I slowly picked up speed. Jack was well ahead when suddenly my front wheel started to wobble, and before I could do anything about it – even if I'd known what to do – the handlebars dropped, twisting violently to starboard at the same time, and I parted company with the tipping saddle, describing a graceful arc that covered something like fifteen feet, before making a wheels-up landing on the back of my neck.

Slowly, the earth stopped gyrating, and as I climbed to my feet, I saw Jack turning, no doubt wondering why he was now alone. Just to tempt fate further than usual, I was wearing the new suit I had treated myself to with my demob pay, and the jacket was ruined. Having landed on the back of my neck, the considerable friction of the concrete surface frayed the worsted through to the lining. In addition, the shirt underneath was likewise rubbed away, as was my skin. These injuries, added to a large bump on the back of my head and a twisted knee, rather spoiled the glory of the morning. I walked slowly home, pushing the bike and mentally vowing that it was the last time I ventured forth on less than four wheels, a vow I have been at pains to keep.

At the end of the week, having given it a little thought, I went up to the Mullard (formerly Philips) factory and applied for work. Barbara Castle had been instrumental in bringing the plant to Blackburn shortly before the war, and I had heard that good money could be earned there, that there was potential advancement within the company, and it was clean work – a 'dressed-up' job. Why not? I had already done time in a cotton warehouse, an engineering firm, cinemas (three) and a dairy, not to mention a few weeks as a window-cleaner, so why not try something completely different?

There was no problem getting taken on, and I was set to work on valve assembly, where men and women sat at long benches and fitted the tiny components that made up the old radio valves. It wasn't difficult and the job was clean, but I still had a lazy eye. Having previously been issued with glasses whilst at school, I had kicked them into touch. I could do all the things necessary and had passed the stringent Forces medical. But this sort of work was different, in that we worked under the glare of Anglepoise lamps, and the components were very small. Some of them had to be held with fine tweezers and spot-welded, and I lost count of the number of times I welded the points of the tweezers together. Every time this happened the foreman ground them down past the welded part, and re-sharpened them, but as time went on, the tweezers, which had started life at something like six inches in length, were reduced to about three. And as no one else seemed to weld their tweezers together, I reasoned the fault must lie with me. I hadn't really settled, anyway, so, when, a few weeks later, Jack told me about a vacancy at the Palace (where he was now Second Projectionist), I gave notice and returned to cinema work, following the old adage about the devil you know.

There was a new manager, Mr Jackson, a very affable man of wide experience, much of it down south in the bigger cinemas. He was full of ideas. One of these he, or rather we the projection room staff, put into effect at Christmas. In his younger days, he had attended the Chelsea Arts Ball and had been most impressed by the cloud of balloons that descended onto the revellers on the stroke of midnight, heralding in the New Year. He outlined his plan to us, to inflate a couple of hundred balloons, take them up into the loft, string them across the dome and release them in the interval during the last performance on Christmas Eve. We listened with mounting horror to this wild idea, knowing as we did the difficulties in merely manoeuvring in the dark, dusty, and extremely dangerous loft area. And to do this while carrying a couple of hundred balloons seemed impossible. But he was adamant, and having given us the outline, he considered his job done. Which it was.

We inflated balloons until we were greying out like pilots pulling out of a tight turn. Just the three of us; Jack, myself, and Billy, the young rewind boy who was the only other full-timer. The McNaughten Vaudeville Circuit, having enjoyed tremendous profits during the thirties and war years, were now cutting back on staff to save a few pounds. The Chief, Mr Smart, found our efforts amusing, though such activities and exertions were, of course, below his dignity.
 As a young man, Mr Smart had enjoyed a long and successful career as a professional footballer with Aston Villa, and he and his partner, a man named Mort, often represented England at International level. In the twenties, he had won a FA Cup winner's medal with the Villa, which he once showed to me as he described an incident in the semi-final against Sunderland (then known as the 'team of all the talents'). The Sunderland star was the incomparable Charlie Buchan, and with Villa leading by the only goal, and the

referee looking at his watch, Buchan, with the ball at his talented feet, bore down on goal. Smart was a gifted talker, and I was imagining the scene, seventy thousand fans holding their breath, the vast ground hushed. All attention focussed on the inevitable duel between Buchan and the Villa 'keeper, the Villa fans praying for the whistle, the Sunderland fans praying for time.

'What happened?' I asked, and Mr Smart gave a smile. The fact that he possessed only one tooth, and that being in his lower jaw, gave this smile a sinister aspect, as I would have imagined that of Sweeney Todd as he stropped his razor.

'Oh, I pulled him down, he said, 'just outside the box.'

This, of course, is the professional attitude, and such things have long been known as professional fouls, although as the rules apply to the game at all levels, I could never understand its acceptance.
'He would certainly have scored,' went on Mr Smart, his tooth fairly gouging his upper lip, 'but we cleared the free kick and went on to win the Cup.'

'And what did Buchan do?' I asked, imagining what I would have done.

'Oh, he was a gentleman, said Mr Smart. 'He just looked at me and smiled and shook his head.'

And Mr Smart looked at me and smiled his sinister smile. Well, you couldn't ask a man like that to blow up balloons, could you?

Somehow we did it. We inflated two hundred balloons, cut short pieces of string to tie the necks and form loops, which we then threaded onto a length of fine rope, rather like a clothesline. Then we man-handled the 'cloud' up into the loft without bursting one. Once there, we lay down on the sloping plasterboard sheeting that lined the dome, and inched forward until we could secure each end of the line to a point just above the circle of coloured lamps that illuminated the dome from inside the curled lip. We did this very carefully, as there was nothing underneath us but the front stalls and seventy feet of space, but we did it and retired thankfully to the box, our triumph rather blunted by the knowledge that two of us would have to return later to release them.

Whilst the Pathe Gazette was being shown during the last performance, Billy and I climbed into the loft and inched our way to the line. Now, if we had been better educated, we might have foreseen the action of warm air rising and causing the tethered balloons to turn gently, twisting the little loops as they turned, until they were tight around the line. What we should have done, of course, was tie a metal ring to each loop, and thread the rings on the line, but that was with hindsight. Meanwhile, the plan was to strike the arc of the slide projector and throw the diffused beam to the stage, and the balloons would drift gracefully down through this beam, to drop like a benison onto the amazed and delighted heads of the audience, who would appreciate this grand gesture and call Heaven's blessings upon our worthy heads. We ought to have recalled the cautionary words of a former Burns on the best-laid schemes of certain rodents and homo-sapiens of the male gender.

Billy was at one side, I the other. The Pathe cock crowed, the silks swept gracefully together as the footlights faded in, and I released my end. The theory was that now, with gravity exerting its pressure, the end of the line would fall swiftly, the balloons sliding off like paratroopers jumping from a plane, all in neat and regular order through the arc of descent. In practice, the tightened loops prevented any such thing, and the whole lot, like a long string of multi-coloured onions, swung through the beam, while from below rose a chorus of laughter, boos, jeers and raspberries. Risking my neck, I slid forward and peered down into the stalls at the sea of upturned faces, and for a fleeting moment, almost felt like hurling myself over the edge, but sanity prevailed and I whispered across to Billy to drop his end.

'Can't reach it,' came back Billy's hoarse whisper.

The non-synch was playing, the usherettes were parading with the ice-cream trays, but few were interested in these incidentals while that monstrous polony swung and twirled in the spotlight beam. I crawled over to Billy and reached the knot, but with one hand - the other clinging like a limpet to the nearest joist - I couldn't undo it. I managed to get my pocket knife and open it with my teeth and sawed the line through, and Billy and I retreated from that awful chorus of derision, to the shelter and sanctuary of the box.

The manager was gracious enough to admit that he, if anyone, should have anticipated the problem, and absolved us of all blame. But that didn't stop me having nightmares about falling into a gaping pit, tightly wrapped in a string of balloons.

All through the winter, the manager's ideas department remained dormant, but with the burgeoning spring it rose and stretched and yawned and began to move. On a bright and breezy morning in late May, he paid one of his rare visits to the box to outline another plan. We ran our programme six days a week, three performances daily, on a continuous basis, and he felt the patrons would appreciate 'something live' sandwiched into the matinee, and with this firmly in mind, he had decided we would put on a baby-show.

We suggested an alternative; a bathing-beauty parade, which we felt would attract a bigger audience. After all, who the hell wanted to watch babies being paraded and judged, except mothers, who notoriously believed that *their* child was, without question, the most beautiful, the happiest, the most engaging child ever to bless a parent? Whereas a beauty-show would create something akin to the packed stalls at the Windmill Theatre, with men in shabby raincoats and jam-jar bottom glasses bringing a packed lunch and fighting for front stalls seats. The manager was adamant, however, and he was the boss. Subtle reminders of the fiasco of the ' cloud of balloons' failed to move him, and as he had already engaged the wife of a local dignitary to be the judge, we wondered just why he had bothered to listen to our alternative suggestion.

So we prepared. Mr Smart gave the lie to those who believed that professional footballers were thick in every other sphere and situation. He was a very versatile man, who performed all manner of feats in the running of the cinema. He was a combination of showman, electrician, mathematician and major domo. He rigged up a stand-mike, arranged the schedule, made out a cue-sheet and we were ready.

To our great surprise, that first show went, not only without a hitch, but with a slickness that was close to professionalism, thanks mainly to the lady judge, who, in her long floral dress and huge picture hat, was remarkably like the lady who introduced the Gainsborough films.

At the designated time, we closed the silks, raised the footlights a little, to give a warm glow to the stage, and raised the house-lights part way. The manager, very smart in evening dress and bow tie, strode confidently from the wings, carrying the stand-mike which he set up centre-stage and made the introductions. The lady made her inspection, chose the winner and second and third, the parents and children trooped off, followed by the judge, and the manager reappeared to close the little interlude and return the mike to the wings. Then on with the show. We had to admit that we had been wrong to anticipate trouble. We were wrong in this, too.
All went well until Friday. Now Friday was, by tradition, the Chief's day off, but Jack was more than competent to run the show and normally, everything went well. During the baby-show on that day, I had gone to the snack-bar for a coffee, and was in the foyer on the way back, when the doors from the auditorium were flung open and down the stairs came a throng; mothers, children and the poor lady judge, looking most embarrassed. The column was led by an Amazon with the colouring of a Gypsy and the build of a Russian hammer-thrower. She glared at me where I stood beside the pay-box, trying to emulate one of the Claymen in the old Flash Gordon serial and sink into the wall. She must have known instinctively that I was one of the staff.

'Where's the manager's office?' she demanded, and cravenly, I pointed to the plainly-marked door. The judge, pale and rather trembly, tried to say something, but was brushed aside as the Amazon went to the door and thundered upon it with a fist the size of a York ham.

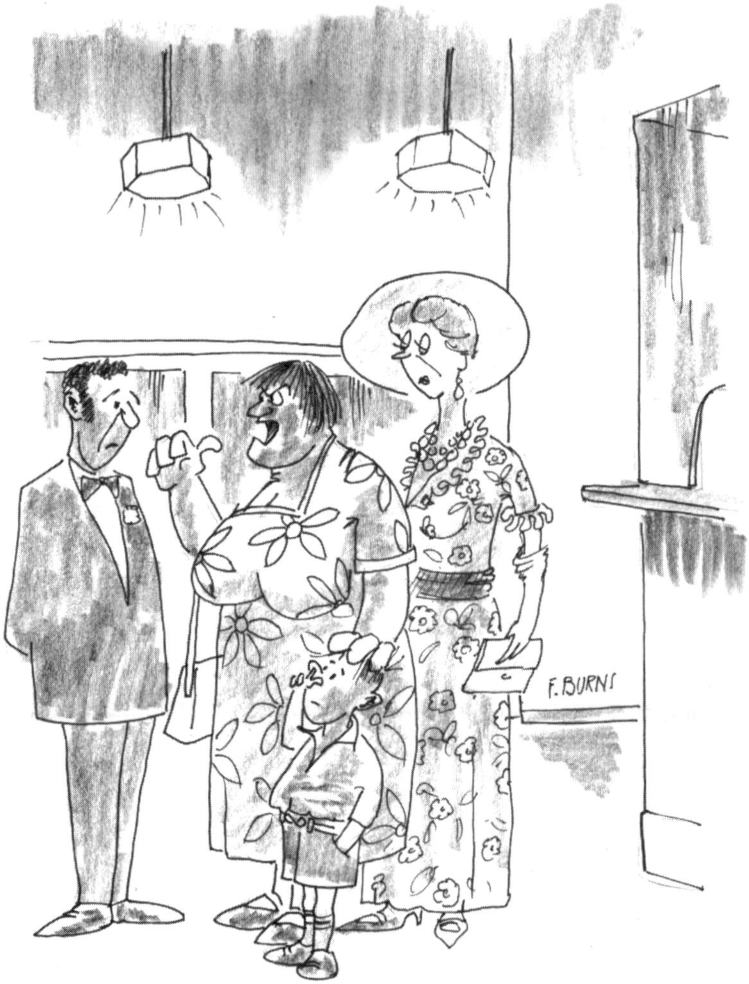
F. BURNS

From behind the door came a strange silence, which reminded me of the poem by Walter de la Mare, the traveller hammering on a sinister door, behind which are 'The Listeners', who maintain absolute silence while quite aware of the traveller's presence and demanding knock. Unlike the traveller, this hammerer did not leave, but hammered again, and this time, after a pause, the door opened and out stepped the manager, a little pale perhaps, but smiling calmly as he explained that he had heard the first summons, but had been engaged in a most important phone-call which he simply couldn't leave. 'Now, what was the trouble?'

The 'trouble' explained the Amazon, was that 'this bugger' – with a jerk of the thumb at the poor judge – had never even looked at her 'bloody kid.' To her eternal credit, the poor judge defended herself against this calumny, only to be silenced by a look of such menace that she faltered into an embarrassed silence. Everyone then looked at the 'bloody kid' who picked his nose unconcernedly.

I take no credit for seizing an opportunity to sidle out and return to the box. I couldn't have helped the poor manager or the judge anyway of course, and, as the show had restarted, I had duties elsewhere. We learned later that the Amazon was set on making the issue public by marching the manager and judge across the Boulevard, to the premises of the local paper, but somehow, this drastic step was avoided, and peace, of a sort, returned. We were relieved that this was the last day of the baby-show. It turned out to be nearly the last day of the Palace.

Jack struck the arc of number one projector, opened the shutter, and called for the tabs to be opened. The white silks began to sweep back as the certificate for the feature appeared on the screen, but, half way, they stuck.

'*Tabs,*' shouted Jack, but Billy, who had thrown the switch, and was now jiggling it up and down, reported that nothing was happening, as we could see. I was operating the stage and house lighting, and had faded all down as the tabs started to open. Meanwhile, the feature had opened, with the titles running and sound on, and although the image where it was covered by the silks was wavy, it was still plain to see. So Jack, mindful of the adage that the show must go on, and making a snap decision, told us to carry on as normal, and rang on the internal phone to the manager's office to tell him of the situation and to request that he get the key to the backstage area, so that he (Jack) could investigate. Then he dashed off, while we carried on.

To his dismay, Jack was handed a bunch of keys that would have made a Yeoman Warder blanch.

'It's one of those,' said the manager, helpfully.

Grabbing the keys, Jack dashed into the auditorium and down the aisle, while the audience stamped their feet in protest at the wavering image on the screen. Reaching the door that led backstage, he tried a key or two, but it would have taken a long time to find the right one. So he did a Douglas Fairbanks' leap onto the stage, clearing the footlights, raising a round of applause and cheers for his extension of the 'live' entertainment. What the audience didn't know was that he could smell something burning, and as he disappeared behind the tabs, he saw smoke. This was issuing from the motor that operated the tabs, and which was still grinding away. Jammed between the pulley and the cable was the stand-mike, which the tabs, in their backwards sweep, had caught and knocked over.

Removing the mike allowed the motor to complete its task, the tabs opened, the show went on and the audience was satisfied. A few minutes more and the motor would have burst into flame, and with the backstage area being tinder-dry, there could very well have been a fire that may have caused casualties and perhaps destroyed the cinema.

There was more to cinema work that running films. There was an 'up' side to this, for the manager, in a rare moment of self-reproach, told us that if he ever broached 'novelties' again, we were to say to him the chilling words 'Baby-Show', and this we swore we would do. He was a good manager, and had only the interests of his patrons at heart, but his ideas did seem to be either flawed or attended by ill-fortune.

The pay for cinema work had never been in proportion to the long, unsocial hours or the degree of responsibility. Not long after the baby-show, we had a visit from one of the directors, a Mr Tatton, who bore a close resemblance to Charlie Chase, but was far less benign. He wandered around, keeping his own counsel and departed, leaving the poor manager to give us the results of his probing. Not content with three complete shows a day, we were now to run the feature *four* times. This meant that our normal working day, of something like twelve hours, would be extended to thirteen plus. And to rub salt into this already-smarting wound, the free 'staff' teas, taken in the café kitchen, were to be discontinued. We were to *buy* our tea in the café, just like the regular patrons.

Mr Smart, who perhaps would have resisted this meanness, had left to take up a managerial post at the Palace's sister show, the Savoy, and Jack was now Chief and I was Second. When we were informed of this front office decision, we were irate. Extending the show time was bad enough, but to scrap the tea we considered to be a breach of contract, as the job, when advertised in the local press, had stipulated this as part of the arrangement, a 'perk' or 'make-weight' to offset the low pay.

Mr Jackson, the manager, was sympathetic and embarrassed to be the one to tell us, but we, for our part, gave him an ultimatum. We would, of course, run the extra feature, but we would not spend our hard-earned money in the café. Instead, we would take an hour off and go home for the meal, and a part-timer could be brought in to cover. (That would cost more than the price of a meal). Furthermore, as we considered the abolition of the free tea to be a breach of contract, we demanded a rise of one pound per week to compensate. (At that time, Jack, as Chief, was paid a little over four pounds per week, and I, two pounds odd).

We expected a decision within the week. If the demands were not met within that time, then the week would count as our notice and we would leave after the final performance on the Saturday. This was Monday morning. Three days later, we got the reply from head office. We were offered a rise of ten shillings, which we rejected. During the war, with the population desperate to escape from the stress and worry, if only for a few hours, the cinemas had been goldmines, and the Palace, with its two-thousand seats, had often played to full houses. The bosses must have been raking in a fortune, and to begrudge the very people who made all this possible was disgusting. And so, not without reluctance, especially on Jack's part, come the Saturday, we stripped the programme, carried the cases downstairs, locked the Dandy Walk door and handed in the keys. The Palace, as far as we were concerned, was history.

CHAPTER NINETEEN

Dyeing For A Living

On Monday morning, we went to the dole and were handed cards to attend for an interview at the Bastwell dye-works premises of Messrs Hodgson and Taylor's. We'd never heard of anything like this, but we needed work and off we went. It was early June, the weather was great, and whatever the outcome of our actions, we would not be cooped up in a projection room on this fine evening. We were shown into the dye-house, or rather one of the dye-houses that made up the complex, and there were met the Dyer, Eric Waywell, and his assistant, Eric Strong.

My first impression of the place was not good. Whitewashed walls reminiscent of Victorian workplaces were enhanced by the men who worked in pairs at long wooden 'becks,' amid an atmosphere of steam and chemical smells. And the floor was wet and all the men wore clogs and rough aprons made of sacking around their waist. It was a like a time-warp, but gradually, as we were shown round by the Dyer, my first impressions became less alarming, and when we saw the way that plain grey yarn was made bright and colourful, we held a short council and decided we would have a go. Especially when Eric Waywell casually told us the rate of pay. More than twice as much as I had been paid at the cinema! And we would finish at five! And no weekend work! As we walked home, we discussed this turn-up and suddenly felt very optimistic, although we *would* need to buy a pair of clogs, which we hadn't worn since schooldays, and a lunch-box. We returned to the Labour Exchange, told them we would be starting on the following morning and went home to organise the clogs and lunch-boxes.

What a happy decision it turned out to be. There was a great deal of interest in the work, variety too, and the workforce, with only a couple of exceptions, were great to get on with and made every allowance for the fact that we had never done anything like this before. We had a full hour for dinner, and while some of the older men rested, we young ones played football on a piece of land that separated the dyeworks from the British Needlefelt works.

In those days, there were still old-fashioned processes in some jobs and hank-dyeing was one of them. The yarn, in hanks, was first boiled in kiers, which were like huge pressure-cookers, then put on sticks, four to a stick, and 'scutched' at a T-shaped pillar, until any kinks were straightened out. We worked in pairs, one each side of the beck, which was filled with water heated to 122 degrees Fahrenheit, into which the colour was diluted. The dyeing was mainly 'vat' where the dyestuffs were made into a solution with caustic soda and hydrosulphate. The hanks were then 'travelled' through the liquor, picking up the colour as they went, turned thirty degrees or so, and the process repeated until the hanks were evenly dyed and dried and samples matched exactly the sample supplied by the customer. The colour might be 'put on at twice' (half of the colour for the first run, half for the second), and extra runs might be needed before the Dyer was satisfied, then the plug of the beck was pulled and the hanks left to drain and oxidise over the empty beck before being thrown up onto a bed of spare sticks laid across the beck. The hanks were then put through a bath of cold water and thrown up again, and a bath of Lensex and soda ash prepared, into which the hanks were then rolled and washed. The last process was a rinse in cold water, after which the hanks were 'noddled off,' laid on a barrow, and wheeled to the 'whizzer,' the huge spin-drier where they were spun and finally taken to be dried out and packed and dispatched.

There were other processes, such as azoic dyeing, used for vibrant shades like red and gold, and applied using the 'nap and base' method. This fascinated me. The grey (sometimes bleached) yarn would go into the first bath known as the nap, so-called because it was composed mainly of naphthalene. Immediately it touched the liquor, the hanks would become a rather weak yellow. After its time in this bath, the hanks would be taken to a wringing-up peg and twisted, using the stick like a tourniquet, until all the liquor was wrung out, then they would be put through the base. Again, the transformation upon the yarn touching the liquor was immediate; resulting in any shade from gold through rust to bright red, and Hodgson and Taylor's ' Rockfast Reds ' were famous in the trade.

There were also sulphur shades, mostly black, brown and navy blue, again very 'fast' shades but all rather variations on the general theme.

We were paid on Friday afternoon, the Dyer bringing around a large wooden tray inlaid with a board drilled with small holes, and in these holes were tiny brass cups with the wages wrapped up in them. As our name was called, we were handed the contents of the cup, while Eric Strong, the Assistant Dyer read out our stoppages, such as National Insurance and income tax. It was all very strange to us, but we liked it and we liked the workforce and were happy. So happy, that the pessimist in me thought it couldn't last.

In January of 1952, I received orders to report for fourteen days reserve training at Number 37 Fighter Auxiliary Unit at RAF Bowlee, Middleton, near Manchester. So dutifully, I packed my things in my kit-bag, donned uniform again and duly reported. I was quite pleased to meet up with a couple of familiar faces at Bowlee, Bob Hendricks whom I had met on the clerical course, and Les Thompson, an old Bridgnorth pal, who lived not far away, in Pendlebury.

I was detailed for work in the Orderly Room, where Sergeant 'Charlie' Peace reigned. Peace was a regular. Tall, balding and with a quiet humour that bordered on satire. There were two erks in the Orderly Room, where a sort of suppressed anarchy reigned. The three eyed me up as I reported, but there was no enmity in the eyeing, merely curiosity. I was probably the first Class 'H' reservist they had set eyes on, and they might have expected to find I had three eyes or two heads or something, and when they realised I was very much like ordinary airmen, they relaxed and we got on well.

'Can you type?' asked Charlie, who insisted on this appellation, and would bristle if addressed by his rank.

'Well, my main job while I was in,' I said, as if somehow I wasn' t 'in' then, 'was cutting the stencils for orders and PORs.'

The other two swivelled to gaze at me in awe, while Charlie did a double-take and his eyes glazed over. I could only assume that the standard of typing had fallen since my day.

'Well, you're just the bloody man we need here,' he said, pushing me towards a desk on which stood an Imperial typewriter, an 'In' tray that was overflowing with documents, and an 'Out' tray that was virginal in its emptiness.

'That lot,' said Charlie, indicating the 'In' tray, 'have to be submitted to GHQ p.f.q. so I'll leave them in your capable hands. Don't raise your head until they are all done, or I shall lop it off cleanly and with micro-precision. Sustenance will be brought and pushed under the door from time to time and while you toil, you can think of the many blessings Allah will visit upon your unworthy head. That is, if it survives the aforementioned lopping. OK?'

Well, Charlie talked my language, and in a very happy frame of mind I set to work. At 10.00 hours I was invited to accompany them to the Naafi.

'Merely jesting, re the grub under the door bit, of course,' said Charlie, as we walked warily on the icy road. It was bitterly cold and the previous falls of snow had partly thawed and then frozen over, making the going extremely dangerous. Leaving us at the Naafi, he departed to join his cronies in the Sergeants' Mess, reminding us that the break ended at 10.15 hours precisely and we were to be back, slaving away like Bob Cratchitt by 10.17, an instruction that was ignored.

'Don't take any notice of Charlie,' said one of my new comrades, nobody else does, except the officers. They think the sun shines out of his arse.'

I pondered about this. The man was certainly no martinet and the neglected stack of returns and official letters and notices seemed to suggest that he ran a slack ship, but I was soon to find out why the officers held him in such esteem. It was a telephone call that did it.

Charlie picked it up on the first ring.

'Orderly Room, Sergeant Peace speaking.'

A long pause, while he listened, motioning me to stay the clatter of the keys.

'Yes sir. At once sir.'

Pause.

'You may indeed, sir.'

Pause.

'No problem whatsoever, sir. Leave it with me, and rest assured you will not be disappointed. Yes indeed, sir.'

A low chuckle.

'And you too, sir.'

Charlie replaced the receiver and his smile disappeared instantly. 'You can ---- off.' he said flatly.

It was so funny I had to laugh aloud, although Charlie remained po-faced. I could imagine the officer at the other end of the line replacing his phone and thinking 'what a damned dependable chap Charlie is, and so *respectful*, too.'

'The bloody fool will forget what he wanted by dinner time,' explained Charlie.

By early afternoon, I had completed the typing and filled the 'Out' tray, while the other two had been off on mysterious errands and Charlie had been deep in a paper-back.

'What's next then?' I asked.

Charlie raised his well-shaped, balding head, a puzzled expression in his eyes.

'Next?' he repeated, then lowered his feet to the ground and dropped the book onto the desk. He stared at the 'Out' tray then shifted his gaze to the empty 'In' tray.

'What have you *done*?' he demanded, in apparent horror.

'Oh my God', I thought, 'I've dropped a clanger somewhere, but I didn't know where.

'There was three bloody *week's* work there, Robbie. Are you stark, raving *mad?*'

He picked up the documents and shuffled through them before dropping them back into the tray. He was shaking his head sadly, but managed to give me a brave little smile.

'With all respect, Robbie, you mustn't work like that. For one thing, it's bad for the health and for another it's setting a dangerous precedent My two lads will never forgive me if I let you do this. They have carved out a comfortable little niche for themselves. and you, unless I can wean you away from this suicidal tendency, will spoil the whole bloody thing. Put half, no, better three quarters, of those docs back in the in tray, put one into the machine and look busy with a pen and paper if any officer shows his face. In the meantime, there's a couple of Hank Jansens in Hibbel's desk drawer.'

We all had a thirty six hour pass that weekend, and as it happened, Bury, just a few miles away, were at home to Blackburn Rovers in an

FA Cup-tie. One of my new comrades in the billet was Lofty Taylor, who lived in Abbey Village, a few miles from Blackburn, and he suggested we take in the match and see if we could get a lift to Blackburn afterwards. With thousands of supporters following the Rovers, we thought our chances were pretty good, although there were far fewer cars in those days.

It wasn't far to Gigg Lane and we enjoyed the game, which Rovers won, then set about looking for a lift, but of all the vehicles parked around the ground, the only one bearing a Blackburn registration was a small Ford van. We waited for about ten minutes until the driver showed up and asked about a lift, but he told us he was staying the evening with friends.

'Never mind,' said Lofty, 'we can get the train.'

We made our way to the station, but when we arrived, there was chaos. The footbridge over the line had collapsed, plunging a lot of people onto the tracks beneath. Whilst we waited, the Rovers mascot, a man by the name of Steve Cryer, was carried past, sitting on a stretcher, wearing his well-known raincoat and long blue and white scarf, and waving his rattle. Both of his legs had been broken in the fall, and poor Steve died soon after. Had we not waited that ten minutes for the van driver, who knows but what we might have been injured?

My period of 'training' was to end at 08.00 hours on Monday, and as we again were free from Saturday noon we Class 'H' lads decided to hand in our bedding, reasoning that the RAF would not make us return merely to sleep the Sunday night and leave first thing after muster parade on the Monday. As we trundled along, an RAF policeman appeared in the door of the Guard Room. Shades of Padgate.

'Class H?' he demanded, and we answered in the affirmative.

'Where are you taking the bedding?'

We explained about the thirty six and the pointlessness of returning to camp for one night.

'Get those blankets returned to the billet,' we were instructed, 'and make sure you're back here by 23.59 hours tomorrow. Where d'you think you are, Butlin's?'

So we returned the bedding and returned to camp on Sunday evening and right after breakfast on the following morning, we left. I decided that if I were summoned again to waste two weeks in like fashion, I would quietly burn the papers. In the event, I was never summoned.

I had always had a gut feeling that the happy days at the dyeworks couldn't last, and I was right. Not long after I returned from reserve training, we were addressed by Eric Waywell. Mr Hodgson, the senior and sole surviving partner, had died a little while before Jack and I were taken on, and although the staff had carried on as normal, completing orders and processing new ones, they had reached the end of the line, and we were all to look for other work. There would be only a week or two's grace, and he hoped in that time we would find work.

Well, there it was. We were very sad at this turn of events, especially as jobs were hard to find at that time, with the Attlee administration now out of office, the new Conservative government were busily refurbishing the Labour Exchanges, ready for business. Jack and I parted company. I was sent for an interview at the Bridge Mill Rubber Company on Moorgate Street, while Jack and another man were sent to Messrs Monk, the tripe dressers.

I didn't care much for the rubber works, because there were such a lot of women, but as the supervisor showed me round, I heard my name called, and looking for the voice, I saw my cousin Florrie, Uncle Tom Bamford's daughter. Florrie's husband, Joe Heywood, had died of wounds in Holland in September of 1944, and Florrie had been left with four children, all at school. The three eldest would be working by then, but Florrie still needed to work to pay for the clothing and things, for her war widow's pension was a disgusting pittance. The supervisor smiled.

'Oh, you know somebody then?'

'Yes, Florrie.'

I went over and talked to her, while the other women, who ranged in age from late teens to late forties, eyed us curiously.

'Are you starting here?' asked Florrie.

Well, I had been about to turn it down, but caught by surprise, I found myself nodding.

'Oh, you'll like it here,' said Florrie, 'It's home from home.'
Well, it wasn't *quite* that, but it was all right, and once I had got over my natural shyness with the women, I quite enjoyed it. My main duty was to go downstairs and across the yard to the 'clicking' room where the soles and heels were clicked from a rubber sheet. I then had to set them up in piles for the women, who smeared raw latex onto the back part of the soles, which then passed through a sort of heated tunnel, where the latex thinned out under the heaters. At the other end, the women took the sole and pressed the prepared heel into position before being passed along to the next stage. With this and keeping the place generally tidy, the work was light enough and I settled in.

I was pleased to find that they ran a football team in the local Combination, and when it was known that I had some experience in goal I was wooed unashamedly until I signed for them. The team was run by Joe Quinn, who, when necessary, was manager, secretary, treasurer, coach and stand-in player. We shared a 'ground' with Newman's slipper works, the term 'ground' being applied loosely, for while there is no doubt that we played on the ground, the venue was merely a meadow on farm land at the rear of Scotland Bank, where the St Andrew's Primary School stands today.

There was a dip running diagonally across the pitch, which was so deep that our outside left, Jimmy Gregson sometimes disappeared from view, although I could hear his eager voice calling for the ball. Poor Jimmy. He was a very nice lad, the soul of geniality and immensely popular. One night, on his way home after a night out, he paused to light a cigarette near the Dun Horse pub and someone mistook him for another with whom he'd quarrelled. As Jimmy bent over his cigarette, he was punched in the face and, falling backwards, his head struck the stone windowsill of the Dun Horse pub and he died as a result. We were depressed for weeks at this tragedy, and disgusted when the original murder charge was reduced to manslaughter.

There were less tragic incidents; like the time the ball ran for a goal-kick, and as time was pressing and we were trailing, I ran to retrieve it from the top of the heap of hay where it had rolled and stopped. The heap was about three feet high, and I leaped to the top with all the exuberance of youth and the panic of knowing we were fast running out of time. But I had made a mistake. The heap was not of hay, but of fresh hen manure, into which I sank to the tops of my stockings. The up-side was that I was given plenty of room when we dressed after the game.

We were on a shoestring, and at one time we even had to buy a new ball on instalments, but we were happy, even though we were in the lowest (fifth) division. We were a 'mud' team. Mud was a great leveller, making life just as difficult for the good players as for the others. And on mud we did very well. We enjoyed our football, and in that first season we reached the semi-final of the St Thomas' Medal Competition. There were two main medal competitions in the town, St Peter's (Mill Hill) being the other, and as the season progressed, especially the final, crowds of a few thousand would turn up to watch.

That first season we defeated teams such as Blackburn Transport and Hospitals, but lost three goals to six against 'Harrison's Gym' in the semi-final. We were disappointed, for the medals were gold and well worth winning, though we were compensated by winning promotion to the fourth division. But by this time the job situation was in a state of flux, and one day we were all called together by one of the directors and told we were being laid off, as the orders were not coming in. With no other prospects, some of us had to sign on at the dole, and I found myself following in father's footsteps and wondering why our sort were always bottom of the heap. I was on the dole for about five weeks, and then one morning I received a letter inviting me to return to the rubber works, but in a different capacity. The work would be in the mill-room, where the raw materials were milled into the rubber sheets from which all the components were cut, and it would be on a two-shift basis, twelve-hour day, alternating with twelve hour nights. With nothing else in view, I could do nothing but agree, and on the first day I reported, the first thing I saw was a labourer washing a Bentley saloon, the newly-acquired property of the director who had announced the laying-off.

I was determined to look for something else, and as things turned out, an incident occurred that precipitated my search.

I was set to work on a milling machine, where the ingredients were mixed and milled between red-hot steel rollers, and we had to cut and peel off the finished sheet and roll it as the mill turned. To reach the top of the rollers was a long stretch, and being on the short side, I had to duck under the bar that operated the clutch and a safety device. If a hand was pulled into the rollers as we leaned *over* the bar, which was just touching our chest, our body would automatically press on the bar and the clutch would immediately disengage and the rollers would stop. That was the theory, and with a tallish man, it would work fine. But both I and the man on the opposite shift, a Ukrainian named Michael, were on the short side. When I arrived one night, I was told that there had been an accident on the morning shift. Poor Michael had ducked under the bar and while cutting the rubber, his hand had been pulled in between the red-hot rollers, and in panic, he had tried to pull the hand free with his other hand, which also had been pulled in. Only by the fact that the foreman was working on the 'Banbury' mixer, high above, saved what could have been so much worse. The foreman leapt down and pushed in the clutch, and eventually the rollers were parted, but Michael lost two or three fingers off each hand.

This incident made me determined to leave as soon as possible, and quite by chance I heard about a job going in Harry Heath's foundry, just at the bottom of Pink Street. I went down there, saw the boss, and was taken on. I started there and then, to hell with the week's notice at the rubber works.

Harry Heath senior had been a foreman moulder. He took over the former stables at the bottom of Pink Street, and almost single-handedly converted it into a foundry. The stables had housed the horses of Doctor Lees, who lived at the bottom of Griffin Street, and thus the area became known locally as 'Physic Brow' (pronounced 'brew'). His house was later converted into the 'Witton Bank Hotel,' later becoming a residential retirement home. Sadly it is now closed.

With a small workforce, mainly composed of relatives and neighbours, the foundry made steady progress, and at one time employed ten people, no little accomplishment for so small an enterprise. But by the time I joined in 1952, there were just three moulders, Harry senior and his two sons, Harry and Jimmy, a furnace-tenter named Bill Pickering and myself, the iron-dresser.

There was a small yard where Bill broke up the items of cast iron that had been bought as scrap. The pieces were thrown up onto the concrete staging, through which the stack of the furnace protruded and which also held the pile of coke with which the furnace was fed, and the limestone chippings that were used at the end of each 'charge' to clear the slag.

On casting days, Harry senior would light the fire in the furnace, and when all was ready, I would take a spade and climb onto the staging, from where I would charge the furnace on Harry senior's instructions, shouted through the open shutter of the moulding shop. Four spadefuls of coke, followed by twenty two of iron and one of limestone chippings, the charge repeated until the casting was completed, when I would go down to the moulding shop and help to remove the hot castings from the moulding sand, then water down the sand. The castings were taken to the dressing-shop and left to cool overnight.

Casting was very hot work, and you never saw a fat moulder. We sweated profusely, especially in the summer months, and, after a cast, one could take off one's shirt and literally wring it out. On the morning following a cast, I would knock all of the runners from the smaller castings and load the ancient rattle-box, throwing in the runners to assist in the rattling. It was rather like putting potatoes into a peeling machine, all the castings being tossed around until the loose sand and little sharp bits were worn off. I would then empty the rattle-box, re-fill it, and, whilst it was spinning, would complete the dressing of the first load, using the grindstone that was being driven from the same shaft as the rattle-box. It was very dirty work, the air full of fine sand and iron-dust, and my nostrils were permanently blocked. But it was also satisfying to take these new pieces that had once been so much scrap iron, and to give them the final dressing and stack them ready for collection by the customers.

We made a lot of fire-grates and frets, which were sent away to be vitreous-enamelled. It was the age of the all-night burning grate, with Firemaster and Sofono being the two most popular ones. But we also made a product that had been the brainchild of Jimmy, and (I suppose as a reminder of the foundry's beginnings) was called the Lees grate. I always thought that this was superior to the Firemaster and Sofono, because for one thing, it required no cementing into the hearth, and for another, the grate itself was a solid frame fitted with loose fire-bars, which could be cheaply replaced when they warped through long use. With the others, the whole grate had to be changed.

The moulding was a fascinating process, and the three were experts. Using either a wooden pattern or one of the actual items supplied by the customer, the moulder would select a 'box', place the pattern in, and cover it with moulding sand, ramming it firmly all round until it was packed solidly enough to enable the box to be lifted and upturned. Then 'parting' sand would be sprinkled over the flat surface, which now had the pattern firmly embedded, and the top half of the box would be put in place, filled with moulding sand and rammed firm, after which, the top half could be lifted off and the pattern removed. When the top half of the box was replaced, there would be a perfect mould of the pattern in the middle, with a hole from the edge to the surface. Molten iron would be run into the hole until it was full, and this bit, the contents of the hole, was the 'runner', and would be knocked off in the dressing process.

Loose pattern moulding was a very fine craft, and the bigger castings often necessitated the running of four ladles in a simultaneous and controlled flow, and the heat rising from the iron would blister an unclosed hand, as I would later discover.

While I was busy with the dressing, Bill would be re-lining the inside of the furnace with ganister, a dreadful composition like wet clay with gravel mixed in. This used to be delivered in the back alley at the rear of the foundry and had to be thrown over the wall into the compound. The wall was about seven feet high, and the ganister used to cling to the spade, the blade of which we had to keep wetting in the water-butt. It was horrible stuff, but necessary to withstand the heat of the blast-furnace.

Bill's job was to re-line the furnace, coat the ladles with damp moulding sand, and edge the lip with clay-wash. In between times, he chopped wood for the lighting of the furnace and broke up the items of scrap. When we cast, he would 'tap out', which entailed chipping carefully at the mouth of the furnace, which had been packed with coke, to leave just a small gap which was then filled with clay between tappings. Once tapped, the iron would run down the short chute to be caught by the ladles, and when these were full, Bill would 'bott up', using a plug of wet clay on the end of a steel rod, rather like the old ramrod of musket days. After a few tappings, the slag would start to appear, and this was allowed to run onto the floor, where it set like old-fashioned bonfire toffee, and when cold had to be handled very carefully indeed, for the edges, when we broke it with a hammer, were razor-sharp and could – and often did – cut to the bone.

There was much more to moulding, but the three of them could make just about anything and were true masters of their trade. They were also affable, and working there, although dirty, was a happy experience in the main, but the plant was very old and very primitive and Harry senior was loath to buy new, which often led to a battle of words between him and Jimmy. When such a battle was in progress, it was both wise and amusing to remain firmly on the outside and listen to the barbed shafts flying across the moulding floor.

Harry junior had been a very useful footballer in his younger days, and could easily have turned pro, but he loved the foundry. On one occasion the then manager of Blackpool came personally to the foundry and spent an hour trying to persuade him to sign full-time, but he declined. He had had trials with League clubs such as West Ham, but remained true to his principles and eventually played for Nelson as a part-time Pro, so that he had the best of both of his worlds.

Harry, and his wife Ivy, lived on Selborne Street, with their three daughters, Ivy, Wendy and Fay, and both he and his wife loved football. I was playing for St Joseph's at that time, and on match days, at their invitation, I would call round and there would be a hot bath ready for me, and tea and cake afterwards, while we sat in the comfortable living-room and discussed football. They were a wonderful couple, two of the finest and nicest people I ever knew, honest and content in their lives and each other, generous and welcoming to everyone, and I feel privileged to have known them.

I had been about three years at the foundry. I enjoyed the work and got on well with my mates, but it was an unhealthy environment. I had suffered with pleurisy when I was younger, my chest was always suspect, especially in the winters, and after casting I would be going out into the often frosty air, still sweating from the cast, and so, with real regret, I decided I had to leave.

Pink Street foundry was demolished in 1974, to make way for an industrial estate, and of course, that was the end of it. Except for one thing. I knew Harry junior loved the place, and many years later, when I was trying my hand at painting, I painted a picture of it completely from memory and gave it to him. Time had erased some of the details from my memory, but sometime later I had a visit from Harry, who had an old snapshot of the foundry taken some time in the thirties, at a time when he had actually lived in the end house, next door to the foundry.

He asked me if I would paint another picture, with a request that I painted the dates 1919-1974 on the gate. This I did. I also typed out a short resume of the life of the foundry as I remembered it. I think he wanted it as a birthday present for one of his daughters, and not long afterwards, he phoned and commissioned another one, which I was happy to agree to. Although I tried to make him accept both pictures as tokens of the great esteem in which I held him and his wife, he would not hear of it. He was a generous man and a good friend, and when he and Ivy died, I am not ashamed to admit I shed some secret tears.

CHAPTER TWENTY

Wanderings

Jack had worked only one day at the tripe dressers. As children, we had often ate – and enjoyed – tripe, not knowing what it was. But now Jack saw it from a very different perspective. They are, of course, the stomachs of cattle, and were delivered straight from the abattoir, still slimy and green from the detritus of the unfortunate animals' last meal. The processes of boiling and dressing, with the attendant steamy smells and slitherings were more than enough. He and his friend, who had been sent with him, saw the boss at the end of the day and told him they would not be back for day two or any other day.

'You didn't give it much of a trial, did you?' said the indignant boss. The only reply to this was that eight minutes, rather than eight hours would have been sufficient for most people.

Anyway, the upshot was that he was now looking for work again, and was given a card to attend Blackburn Yarn Dyers on Haslingden Road, where he was taken on. When he heard that I was leaving the foundry, he said he would ask for me. I was told to go for an interview, and when the dyer, Don Clayton, found I had a little experience, he took me on.

The plant was much more modern, the dyeing was done either in warps or beams, which obviated most of the manual work of hank dyeing. There were several warp-dyeing machines, ranging from 'The Pup', a single box machine, to the four-box machines used mainly for azoic dyes. With this type of dyeing, the warps, being long coils of raw yarn, were run over a wooden frame that stretched the length of the machine. Running in grooves, the warps were fed in by tying the ends to a 'jack-band', a kind of leader, that remained constantly threaded around the rollers on the machine. Passing from the front of the machine, the yarn went over the frame and down into the first box, following the jack-band over a series of rollers beneath the surface of the liquor, up through a pair of rubber rollers that squeezed out the liquor, and down into the next box and so on, until it had completed the cycle and finally descended via a rotary drum into a large wooden box on wheels. The liquor was applied by pouring part of the mix into the box and feeding the rest at intervals as the yarn progressed, and the art of this type of dyeing was to keep the colour 'level.' Feeding too much, or at too-short intervals, caused the colour to get 'heavier' as the yarn progressed, while too little had the opposite effect.

It was here that I renewed acquaintance with some of the older men from Hodgson and Taylor's, and it was like coming home, in a fashion. The workforce were friendly in the main, and at first I was happy going to work. However things began to deteriorate through no real fault of mine or anyone else's, but the tapestry of life is woven with many and varied threads, and it is necessary here to leave the narrative flow for a moment in order to explain.

Number Three, Pink Street, was the home of the James's, Bill and Susie and their family; Frank, Mary, Jack, Alban, Bill junior and the youngest, Robert, or Bob, as we always knew him. Bob was a couple of years younger than me, but in our early teens, we had struck up a friendship, mainly because we were very similar in temperament and interests. After I was demobbed, we carried on our friendship, as

Bob was serving his apprenticeship at Lonsdale's on Pump Street, and his call-up was deferred until he had served his time.

We were on our way home from a Rovers game one Saturday evening and he went into the newsagent's shop on Whalley Banks, whilst I waited outside. As I waited, a young woman came out of the greengrocer's next door, and I recognised her as Mavis Dean, who had worked at the Palace. She stopped to talk and we made a date. That was in the winter of 1952 and just a year later we were married. No marriage is 'made in Heaven.' Marriage is hammered and wrought at the forge of Life, tempered by adversity and polished by striving to do what's right in any given situation. This isn't always possible, of course, and there are good times and bad times. But whereas today's trend is to call the whole thing off at the first sign of adversity, we were raised to accept bad and good, rough with smooth, and – above all – to put as much as we could into it. We've had ups and downs but on Boxing Day 2003, we will be celebrating our Golden Wedding, so on that note I'll end this little digression, just in case anyone should think I'm preaching.

Things were hard at first, as we had no money, but by the time our first child arrived, we had taken out a mortgage on a terraced house. In those days, most children were born at home, unless there were complications, the pregnancy monitored by the visiting midwives, who were, in the main, splendid. The doctor was only called upon after the birth, to check mother and child. Mrs Livesey was a very competent and friendly woman, and her confidence and common sense helped enormously, especially as it was our first. Our son, who we christened Gerrard Francis, was born on Easter Monday, April 11th 1955, not long after I started work at BlackburnYarn Dyers.

I had always been a heavy sleeper, but with the arrival of Gerrard, my sleep became disturbed. He was very difficult to settle, and would cry far into the night. We took turns to pace the floor with him, often into the early hours so that when we eventually got some sleep, neither of us would hear the alarm, and I would be late for work. Being new parents, we tended to worry that there was something wrong, but he gained weight normally and in every other way, was perfectly normal. It was just that he must have been a born a night-owl while, I of necessity, was a lark. The two were incompatible.

When I first began arriving a few minutes after everybody else, Don Clayton the Dyer, took a liberal view, but as time went on, he spoke to me once or twice and all I could do was promise to try to get in on time. I think he had formed the opinion that I was just naturally both a heavy sleeper and of a lazy nature, and his attitude hardened until one Friday he called me into the lab and closed the door.

'You have a four-hour run tomorrow,' he said, 'and you *must* get here on time.'

Once the run had started, it had to carry on to the end, and as we worked just four hours on Saturday, his point was clear and reasonable.

'I'll be here,' I said.

'Don't let me down, he replied, 'because if you're late, I shall have to put someone else on your machine.'

There was an implied threat behind these soft words. Once we got our 'own' machine, it was an unwritten law that no-one else ran it, and if for some reason another man had to stand in, then he had every right to be considered the permanent man. I could only repeat that I would be in on time, and he accepted this.

That night, as I tried to sleep, the thought kept nagging me that if I was late, I would most likely get the sack, and the more I tried to relax, the more this thought impinged, and by the time I did manage to drop off, it was very late. Even so, I was up in good time, and heaved a sigh of relief as I picked up my lunch-box and set off.
I always walked the two miles, mostly uphill, and I knew I could do it in forty minutes. When the Cathedral clock chimed quarter past seven, I was crossing the Boulevard. Plenty of time. But then doubts began to creep in. I had never really timed myself, and two miles – uphill – was no stroll. As I turned into Bridge Street, the Ribble bus was there, with a couple of men on board and the conductor

lounging near the door. I hesitated. The fare was sixpence, little enough to ensure a nice early start, and probably time for a brew and a smoke, too. But no, I would walk. Plenty of time. Or *was* there? I was dithering, a great failing of mine, and by this time, a couple of minutes had slipped by without my walking a step further, and in moment of decision, I turned back and climbed aboard.

Wrong decision! The conductor looked at his watch and decided he may as well start to collect the fares, while he waited for his driver. An alarm bell ought to have rung, knowing my penchant for being in the wrong place at the wrong time. But if it did ring, I didn't hear it. The conductor issued the first couple of tickets and came to me. I paid him my money and he turned the handle of his machine; that is, he *would* have turned it, but it just stopped dead, and no amount of turning, twisting, or cursing could make it turn. *Now* I heard a faint bell.

'I'll just nip across to the office and change this bloody thing,' said the conductor, and as he left he told us to explain to the driver when he turned up, that he would not be two minutes. I did not have a watch, but I calculated that it must be about half past seven, and sure enough, just then the cathedral clock chimed the single stroke. Could I still make it on foot? I was feeling distinctly uneasy, but as I wavered between waiting and walking - not forgetting the conductor now had my money, *and* my ticket - the driver dashed up, dived into the driving seat, started the engine and looked round for the conductor to ring him off. It was obvious to us that the driver was late, and didn't take kindly to having no conductor.

'Y'mon's gone to change his machine,' said a burly Irishman sitting on the side seat opposite the driver's cubicle. The driver cursed, switched off the engine. We waited.

And waited.

By now, of course, I hadn't a chance of walking and arriving on time, and knowing my luck, I decided that if I did take a chance, it was an odds-on bet that the bus would pass me before I had gone a hundred yards.

'Where the bloody hell as he got to?' demanded the driver, as if we knew. Then he opened the little door, muttered about finding him, and trotted off along the boulevard.

As the driver dwindled from view, the conductor, brandishing his new machine, appeared from under the awning of the *railway* station, leapt aboard and reached for the bell-push before he noticed that the driving seat was empty.

'Where's the daft sod got to?' he demanded.

We were all fed up with this guessing game and maintained a surly silence.

'I'd best go and see ...' began the conductor, making as if to leave.

'No you bloody well don't,' said the Irishman. 'Youse two are like bloody Laurel and Hardy. Stop where you are.' And the glint in his eye brooked no argument.

The conductor, muttering and glowering, subsided onto the front seat, and a minute or two later, the driver was seen, running like an Olympic sprinter, across the Boulevard. He leapt aboard, jumped into his seat while cursing the conductor, who rang off immediately and off we went.

The driver, casting caution to the wind, tried to make up his lost time, and he and the conductor maintaining a running, whispered argument as we rolled wildly around corners and ignored waiting would-be passengers, who shook fists and shouted obscenities as we passed. I couldn't have cared less.

I clocked in at about five minutes past eight - the driver *had* made up some time - and found 'my' machine running happily, with another man at the controls. I didn't wait to be called to the lab, but went and knocked.

'Come in.'

Don's voice was cold and angry, as it had every right to be, and I felt terrible as I went in and closed the door.

'Well?' he asked icily, 'what's the excuse *this* time?'

'You wouldn't believe me if I told you.' I said, and he raised no argument with this. So then and there, I tendered my notice and, with a weary sigh, he accepted it.

'What are you going to do?' asked Jack Pemberton, the man who – most unwillingly – had taken over on the four-hour run.

I had been detailed to fill in the morning doing odd jobs like dyeing samples on 'The Pup' and sweeping the floor. 'I don't know.' I said.

'No chance of stopping on?'

'No.'

'There's a little dye-house on Forrest Street,' he said. 'I worked there for a while. Not as good as this place - which suddenly seemed *wonderful* to me - but it's steady, and the boss is a very decent chap. As a matter of fact, his dad was old Hodgson's partner. It's worth a try. Tell him you worked at Bastwell.'

I went around to Forrest Street, and saw Derek Taylor, who was the very soul of geniality, and when I mentioned that I had worked at his father's old enterprise, I was welcomed into the rather dismal little fold.

The dyeworks, where the old-fashioned hank dyeing was still in vogue, was a rambling old building in a yard that was occupied by some other enterprises, the main one being William Birtwistle's (Damasks). It was from this company that Mr Taylor bought his steam and electricity. I think the dye-house had been the sweets factory of Harry Boyle, a Victorian entrepreneur, and was like something from a Dickens novel, a maze of narrow corridors and dark staircases, where rain dripped and puddled on the flagged floors, and a huge basement kitchen, with an enormous grate where one of the older men kept a great fire of coal and coke burning all day, and where we could cook or heat our meals.

Derek Taylor was by far the easiest-going boss I ever worked for, and although he had been raised a gentleman and educated in Switzerland (or so I was told), there was no edge whatsoever on the man. He would talk happily to us on a variety of subjects, particularly cricket or football, even if it meant we had to stop working to talk. He also had a keen sense of humour and would tell the current jokes with great enthusiasm, laughing heartily, even though he'd heard them before.

The dye-house, which had about a dozen wooden becks, was gloomy, illuminated by bare bulbs here and there. The ancient flag floors echoed eerily to our clogs, for there were only six men, whose primary work was dyeing and waxing khaki yarn for the army, and running thick webbing straps through a protective solution. These were the ammunition belts used on the Besa machine-guns in the tanks of the day. There were other jobs, but with hank-dyeing all but obsolete, not many. But our wages were always there, and were even about ten shillings a week better than the pay I had earned at BYD. Of course, there had to be a snag.

Mr Taylor was forgetful. From time to time we would find that when we turned on the steam valve, nothing happened. Derek had forgotten to pay his account to William Birtwistle and the steam had been shut off. Someone must have got in touch with the boss somehow, and as suddenly as it had stopped, the steam would come through again, but after I had been there a while, the atmosphere became strained, and it was rumoured that the boss was in financial difficulties. Some time later, this fear was confirmed, and once again I was looking for work.

My thoughts turned to Mullard, and one day I took a walk up there and easily got a job in the wire-drawing department. There were long benches made of steel plates bolted to cast iron legs, and it was with a little surprise that I recognised these as the castings we had made at the Pink Street foundry. They were rectangular, about four feet high and three wide and their dressed weight was one hundred and thirteen pounds, as I well remembered! There had been no modern tools at the foundry, and the manner in which I had to dress these was primitive. First I had to brush off the loose sand with a wire brush, as they were far too big to go into the rattle-box; then I chipped of the runners with a hammer and cold chisel, before finishing with a piece of carborundum - portable grindstones were like something from Flash Gordon to Harry senior. For this dressing, I had to lift the casting onto a pair of trestles, and when finished, lift them off and stack them as high as I could 'throw' them, as there was little floor space in the dressing shop. And all in all there was a hell of a lot of weight involved.

I had a week on day-work, to be instructed, and after that, it was twelve-hour shifts, days and nights about, and piece-work. I never did get the hang of this job. First of all, I had to look after ten 'heads', the small machines rather like a rewinding machine in a projection room. A 'slug' of wire of a certain thickness was put on one spindle, the end of the wire sharpened by holding it in a bath of acid, while creating a current by shorting with the pliers against the side of the metal pot, then the end was threaded like cotton through a diamond die. The die was then dropped into a slot in a small oil-bath, the wire pulled through and wrapped around the hub of the empty spool and the motor started. In theory, the wire would then run through the die, which would reduce its thickness and come off at the end, longer and finer, and would then progress down the line of heads until the required calliper was reached. In practice – with me, at any rate – this seldom happened, either because of poor quality wire or faulty dies, and I found that although I was working hard I was making very little bonus and the flat rate wasn't much. Still, with the overtime, I was making more money than I ever had before although after a while I grew to hate the job and dreaded going in.

It was all bed and work. If on the early shift, I had to be up very early, and I came home quite late. After tea, I had only a couple of hours before it was time for bed again, so that I would be up in time for work on the morrow. When on nights, which were seven p.m. until seven a.m., I would set off right after tea and arrive home about eight the next morning. A cup of tea and upstairs, where I slept until about four. It wasn't much of a life, and I saw very little of my wife and son, and after a while I managed to get a transfer to another building.

Here, I tended to a machine that made the bases for valves. Small glass rings were dropped onto a revolving spindle which progressed along the circular bed of the machine in measured beats, while twin gas jets played on the glass until it became molten. Nine small electrodes were then bedded into the soft glass base, which was then cooled until, at the end of the process, it was pushed off the bed and rolled down a metal chute, to be picked up and placed into a wooden tray in which sixty holes were drilled, ready to receive it. The tray was then held under the lamp and angled so that the light would show up any cracks in the glass. It was, like most jobs there, soul-destroying in its repetition, and even eight hours seemed like a hell of a lot longer. But I stuck at it because I had to, although I grew to hate it, and even writing about it recalls the frustration and boredom. But relief was at hand.

Jack called round one evening and said he'd been discussing things with the Dyer, who seemed to be feeling a little guilty over my leaving, although why he should have I couldn't say. Anyway, Jack suggested that if I were interested, it might pay me to go up and have a talk with him, and this I did. I finally got to explain the reason for my final lateness. He was able to see the funny side and so after a little talk, it was arranged that I would serve notice at Mullard, and return to B.Y.D. This was an enormous relief to me. The wage would drop, of course, but I would be working sensible hours in a job I liked.

CHAPTER TWENTY ONE

The Road to The Star

I was put on beam-dyeing, under the watchful eye of Frank Brown, the foreman, and found this different from warp-dyeing although no less interesting. Jack was now the colour-mixer, and he would mix our colour in a large metal drum beside the dye-tank, which held two beams, while we prepared the 'bath'. When this was ready, we would start the pump which forced the liquor through the perforated centres of the beams and so on, through the yarn. Then we would add the rest of the colour, using a half-gallon can and gradually feeding it on. Halfway through the process, the pump was stopped, the beams turned through 180 degrees and the other half of the run completed. The greatest danger was from a wide split opening in the beams, known as 'bursting', through which the colour would pour, instead of seeping gradually and evenly. When this happened, the beam had to be hoisted out and wheeled back to the women who would re-beam it, and the whole process would start again.

The manager was a down-to-earth man named Frank Hodgson, (no relation to the partner of Taylor, at the Bastwell works) and his son Gordon, whom he put through the mill, was very keen on football and played for the old boys of the Grammar School, popularly known as 'Old Blackburnians' or 'Old Blacks.' One summer he entered us in a five-a-side competition played at Oswaldtwistle. We couldn't even raise five men young enough and daft enough, so we conscripted Harold Walmsley, whose father had a haulage business, and who did much of the delivering for B.Y.D.

It was the late fifties, and some workers, notably those in the car industry, were beginning to accelerate from the advancing economic bayonet-charge, leaving the rest of us trailing, especially the textile industry, which had never been well paid. In addition, our regular Saturday mornings had been knocked off. After an approach, Mr Hodgson offered us each a Saturday morning in turn, as the best he could do, and this we accepted. The work would be merely sweeping down the womens' beaming frames and tidying up in general, and there would be two men employed on this in turns. After one of these mornings, the manager felt that the two men who had been in, had not done the job properly. A row ensued, and the outcome was that Jack and the lad who had been his partner, gave notice.

In 1960, Jack started work at Cupal, the pharmaceutical company on King Street, and after a few weeks, he told me there was a vacancy there if I was interested. I hadn't been happy about the way in which Jack had been taken to task over what turned out to be very a very minor incident, involving a little dust and fluff that had been missed, and which was picked up at the termination of the exchange. So I gave notice and left to join him. It was a mistake.

Cupal was an old four-storey building behind what is known as King Street Bridge, but is really Whalley Banks, and the owners were an old-established family with old Victorian ideas of 'master and worker'. The pay was about on a par with B.Y.D, but we were expected to work strange hours, sometimes going back after tea, when a late driver would be there, and we would load his van until late in the evening. Sometimes we would be asked to work on a Sunday, but the rate of overtime was not double time as at most other enterprises, but time and a half. This I refused to do, and there were one or two other abrasive little incidents, and I hadn't been there long when I was sacked for refusing to return after tea. My argument was that we'd completed a day's work and theirs was that the vans were sometimes late returning and that was just our bad luck. Maybe they had a point, but so had I, especially as they were so tight with the money. Anyway, I was given a week's pay in lieu of notice and once again was looking for work. Which wasn't far away.

Loxham's engineering works were at the bottom of Throstle Street, immediately behind Pink Street, where, at that time, we were renting Aunt Mary Ann's old house. They wanted a labourer, and I was taken on. The foreman told me there would be some overtime, but half way through the first – and last – week, one of the fitters told me that the only overtime went to the other labourer. When I approached the foreman for clarification, he hummed and hawed and finally admitted that this was so. Well I told him I would finish on the Friday, and to have my cards ready, and he got a little stroppy and demanded a week's notice. But I told him he wasn't entitled to it and in the end I picked up my cards and money and so completed my shortest engagement. In the meantime, I had been to the Star paper mill at Feniscowles and been offered a job in the 'salle' the finishing room, as a serviceman. By this time, it was the start of the summer 'shut' and it was arranged that I would start on the Monday following the 'start-up'.

CHAPTER TWENTY TWO

Paper Mill Work

The salle was a warm place, even in winter. The humidifiers added to the general discomfort in hot weather, but were necessary to prevent the paper curling at the edges when the air became too dry. There were three production guillotines, two German RPMs and the American Seybold, and an old-fashioned Grieg, a beautiful example of late Victorian engineering, which was too slow for production and so was only used for cutting samples. From the machine-houses, where it was made, the paper went to the cutters, where the long reels were cut into sheets and piled on 'boxes' which were really stillages, then taken to the salle where it was counted into reams or half-reams, sorted, examined and, if required, guillotine-trimmed. Then the paper would be packed and stored in the despatch area, awaiting the lorries that would deliver it to the printers, publishers or manufacturers.

The mill produced several types of paper, mostly for publication – magazines and booklets – and some for labelling products. The grades were known as 'Diamond Star', 'Bronze Star', 'Astralux', 'Litho Label' and 'Litho Publication', and one of the regular orders was for The Reader's Digest. My job would be to bring boxes of paper to the women sorters and examiners, take away the 'broke' (faulty paper) and keep the place tidy, all under the direction of one of the female supervisors, who in turn worked under the direction of the salle foreman. There were about two hundred women in the salle, and some sixty or so men. One of the first men I met was Joe Walton, who had been a boyhood neighbour in Pink Street. He became an apprentice motor mechanic, was called up into the army and then returned to his employer, where he was permanently employed on re-conditioning engines. His pay would have been around ten pounds a week. At the Star, he could double this, with overtime, and I too found I was earning money I had never dreamed of, although this included a great deal of overtime and weekend work.

I soon settled in and although it was a bit strange at first, to be among so many women, I soon got used to it and I liked the job and the people. At first I was on two shifts, mornings 6am to 2pm. and afternoons 2pm to 10pm. The day workers finished at five, but there were several women, mothers of young children, on the 'twilight' (6-10) shift. There was a happy-go-lucky atmosphere, no one breathed down your neck, and altogether, I was happier than I had been anywhere else.

While I had been drifting from job to job, we had fallen behind with the mortgage repayments and in the end we gave up and went to live with my parents in Pink Street. We had had a lot of bad luck in the house, and I am convinced that there are houses that have sinister or unpleasant vibrations, and that had been one of them. Nothing had seemed to go right for us, and in the end, I for one was glad to leave, even though it meant living with my parents. In the event, we stayed for about three years, and then number six, next door to Aunt Gert, (Aunt Mary Ann's old home) came empty and the landlord agreed to let us rent it and we moved in.

It was like a time-warp; little had changed since aunt Mary Ann's day, and there was still only gas lighting, but we had it wired for electricity, decorated and bought things as we went along, and after a while, it wasn't too bad. Things were looking up.

I must have been satisfactory, for soon I was put on the Astralux section. Astralux was, at that time, very hush-hush, a top quality paper that was finding a new market and doing very well for its inventors. And while it was still new, only the best quality of paper and finishing would do. To operate this section, the best supervisors, examiners and sorters were selected, and I considered it quite a feather in my cap to be put on there. I was on this for quite some time, and then, out of the blue, the foreman asked if I had ever thought of going on packing. Well, I hadn't, to be honest, for the packers were on piece work and seemed to be constantly in a fever, shouting for work or wrappers or something, but it was the top money – apart from jobs like guillotine operating – and I thought it over and finally said I would give it a go.

Packers worked in pairs, each with a permanent mate, and mine was Dick Thornton, a stocky ex-miner with a keen sense of humour and a strong Welsh accent. I was surprised to learn that he was not Welsh, but a native of Blackburn, who had married a Welsh girl after wartime service with the Navy, and had lived in Wales, working in the coal mines. He lived among the Welsh for so long that when he eventually returned to Blackburn, he couldn't understand the dialect. He was a damned good worker and a first class mate.

We spent the first three weeks with two of the day-work packers who showed us the ropes. Like most jobs, it wasn't as easy as it looked, but we picked it up and eventually went onto three shift working, taking our turn on the guillotines. It was when returning from the night shift one Saturday morning that I had a very strange experience, one that defied all logic and must have had paranormal connections.

When I was a youngster, grandma Bamford's sister, Aunt Mary Ann, lived at number six, with her husband Jimmy Walsh and their family; Mary, Bill, Pat, Agnes and Andrew. If I happened to be playing nearby, Aunt Mary Ann would often shout for me to run errands for her, and when I went into the house, there was always a very strong smell that was peculiar to that house alone. It seemed to be a compound of frying fish and tobacco smoke. Staunch Catholics, they had fish every Friday and Uncle Jimmy was very fond of his pipe. As all the cooking was done on the open fire in the front room, and as Uncle Jimmy always sat to the right of the hearth, quietly puffing at his pipe, the commingling was, as I said, peculiar to number six.

Not long after we had moved in, I came home from the night shift and opened the front door, which, like all the others, opened directly onto the street. As I entered there was the very powerful smell of frying fish and pipe tobacco! I stopped in my tracks, and wouldn't have been in the least surprised if I had seen Aunt Mary Ann and Uncle Jimmy by the fire. There was no mistaking the smell, and the hair on the back of my neck rose, but of course, apart from myself, the room was empty and silent in the grey morning light. Mavis and Gerrard were still in bed, and I went quietly upstairs and was soon asleep. When I woke around noon, the house was normal, and I never again smelled it. I can offer no rational explanation and do not intend to try.

Beside the paper mill was a small council estate, and the land on which it was built had been bought from the paper mill owners, so their workers were given priority when vacancies occurred. I was talking to May Magee, one of the supervisors one day, and she mentioned this to me and when I went home, I told Mavis and we decided to try for a house. At that time, the area came under the Rural District Council, with offices in Wellington Street (St John's), off Preston New Road, and I went down one morning and had a chat and made an application. Well, I thought, perhaps in a year or two, we'll get one of these nice houses with a garden and a bathroom.

By then we had three children, Gerrard, born on April 11th 1955, Christopher, born on 24th September 1961 and Christine, born on 5th September 1964, so we really did need a bigger house. It was only about eight months after applying that I got a letter to say there was a house coming vacant on Coronation Avenue, and if I went to the RDC office, I could take the key and look it over. This I did, and found number thirty to be the middle house of a block of three, with nothing behind but farmland and the Star mill in the bottom. I went home and told Mavis and she told me to tell them we'd have it. The fact that she hadn't been able to see it didn't matter. We moved in on the sixteenth of December 1964.

Many years later some council estates became slums of the worst kind, with people vandalising once-lovely houses and gardens. To people who had been raised in two-up and two-down houses like the one we had, they were wonderful. For the first time, we had a bathroom and indoor toilet, and a back-boiler which gave us hot water. Plus a garden in the rear and a small lawn in front. And two minutes walk away was the Memorial Recreation Ground - The Rec - with space to play football and cricket and swings and slide for the children. Nearby was the great little school, which reminded me a lot of Bank Top. We lived there for thirteen years and for the most part were very happy. Unfortunately, some of the long-term tenants didn't like children and there was the odd argument, but these are part and

parcel of everyday life, although we never did understand why people took exception to children playing properly.
Another bonus was that I was just a couple of minutes walk from work. I could nip over the back garden fence and walk down the field to the top time office in less than two minutes.

The work of packing the reams - or half-reams - was clean, but damned hard, for it was all lifting, and we usually worked twelve hours. In summer, what with the heat and the humidifiers, it was really exhausting, and sometimes the women would refuse to work if it was too hot, and were usually allowed to go home. This option was never shown to the men, but even if it had been, we couldn't afford to lose money. The heaviest 'single-man lift' was the Diamond Star Double Medium eighty three. Double Medium was a paper size of 23 X 36 inches, and each ream weighed, as the title implied, eighty three pounds. A few hours on this, lifting the reams to the bench, packing them in three wrappers and then lifting them onto a box, stacking them as high as you could reach, was hard on arms and back. By contrast, the Double Royal size, of 25 X 40 inches was deemed by the union to be a 'two-man lift', although these reams were usually much lighter. It didn't seem logical to me, and I can only assume that the four-inch extra in length was the deciding factor.

In the spring of 1965, I had been at the Star for nearly five years, and had been happy, but things were about to change. A time and motion study team had been brought in to re-time all the piece-work jobs and this proved to be a disaster for the packers. Packing was carried out in three different ways: bench-packing, when the reams had been counted and examined and 'piled down' on boxes, guillotine packing, when we worked with the guillotine team, packing the reams as the operator swung them onto the plate, and 'examining', where we worked with either one or two girls, packing the reams as they completed the counting and examining. Of the three systems, the last was the best paid, with guillotine packing second and bench packing a poor third.

The Time and Motion people spent about three weeks with us and then one day we were asked to go in an hour early so that the new timings could be explained to us. It was a farce. We were given three work-sheets, to show us how we could earn very much better money under these new timings – once the union had agreed and ratified them – and while trying to take in these figures, we were also expected to listen to one of the team explaining other things, and between the two, we really didn't have time to make a proper study.

'Two of these work-sheets are the actual sheets from two of the packers,' explained the T and M man, 'and you can see the sort of bonus they made by working diligently.'

I noted that the two sheets in question were for examining and guillotine packing, and I asked about the one for bench packing. The T and M man went into a long spiel about why they had been unable to produce an *actual* sheet, but he assured us the sample they had 'assimilated' was about right.

'I'm just looking at these new bench packing times,' I said 'and it looks wrong. If, for instance, we spent eight hours on Double Crown thirty (20 X 30 inches and 30 lbs weight) we would have to pack thirty reams an hour, every hour, before we even started to make any bonus. In other words, we could spend all of a shift packing thirty reams an hour and not make a penny. Is this the reason you couldn't find an actual work sheet? That none of the packers you timed could make any money on bench packing?'

The man next to me was nudging me in the ribs and telling me to leave it, so I listened to the excuse and sat down, and then we were herded out. As we filed out, the man who had nudged me said I'd nearly ruined things by drawing their attention to the sheets.
'Look at these timings for examining,' he whispered. 'They've dropped a clanger here. We'll make a fortune with these timings. We'd best get the union to ratify them before they realise what they've done.'

I told him my suspicions; that they knew *exactly* what they'd done, and that the too-good-to-be-true timings for examining were exactly that. 'They obviously want us to accept the parcel, and the bait is the examining timings,' I said, 'and once we sign up, they'll knock the examining off.'

He grinned. 'They can't do that. Union agreement. They have to keep things as they are.'

'We'll see,' I said.

I'd had a few dealings with bosses and with union officials, and in many cases, they were too close to each other for reassurance. I had a word with the union representative, who assured me that the packers would get a vote before the new timings were ratified, and in the meantime we carried on as normal. After a week or two, I brought up the subject and was amazed and furious to be told that the union had accepted the parcel. There followed the usual double-dealing and reneging, and one afternoon, we refused to start work. The branch secretary of the union came up and tried to sort things out, but failed and in the end we were ordered by management to start work, and if we refused, the overtime would be knocked off.

Now many of the packers were a lot better off than I was, but as soon as this threat was issued, they began to waver. In vain I suggested that we call their bluff, arguing that if we didn't work overtime, the orders wouldn't be met. Then the paper would pile up waiting to be packed, and this would create a backlog in the machine houses and would hurt management more than us, and some solution acceptable to both sides would have to be reached. It was no use; all they could see was a drop in earnings, and the majority caved in. There was no point in the few of us who were prepared to fight going on, and as we left the meeting, I went to the shift foreman and gave two weeks notice. I could no longer work with people whose views were so narrow and whose principles were so easily conquered. And so, just five years after I first entered the mill, I collected my cards. I had never stayed at one place as long, and I was truly sorry to leave, but there was a principle involved, and the bottom line was that I had to find another job. It so happened that Jack, who had been working as a sheet-tester in the mill, had also handed in his notice, and when he called at our house and mentioned this, he also mentioned that the Post Office Telephone people were recruiting, and he intended to apply. I decided to go along.

We attended an interview at Claremont House, and were given a cursory test in reading and a test for colour blindness, which we both passed easily enough. Then we had to go home and wait to be called for a medical examination, which turned out to be as rigorous as the one for the armed forces. But in the end, we were both taken on. Being a Civil Service job, there was a probationary period before being offered the establishment papers, and as things turned out, I only stayed six months.

I was put on one of the 'major works' gangs for a start, and was quite happy, although the pay was not so good (£12.15s). We had been warned at our first interview that overtime was *not* guaranteed, but might become available as time went on. All through the summer I carried on, making up the shortfall in pay from the lump sum I had been paid when I left Star. Though it didn't last long.

I had not been on the job long when we had a terrible scare. In 1965, polio was diagnosed in Blackburn, and we were all urged to take the Salk vaccine. Adults and younger people took the sugar lump with the vaccine added, but babies were given the vaccine as a syrup, on a spoon, and for this, Mavis took Christine, then about eleven months old for the syrup. That evening, Christine was pettish, which was not like her, and Mavis noticed that she wasn't moving her left arm. Concerned, she proffered a biscuit, deliberately urging her to use her left hand to accept it, but the arm didn't move and she reached for the biscuit with her right hand. I thought it was most likely a local reaction to the vaccine itself, because obviously with a vaccine, the disease itself, in a mild, controlled form, was introduced into the system, but Mavis, an excellent mother who never took the slightest chance, was worried and sent for the doctor, who found traces of the polio in her motion and she was taken to Park Lee Isolation Hospital. By this time, she was normal, which seemed to suggest that it was nothing more than a reaction, but she was kept in and we were told not to mingle with people. She spent her first birthday in hospital, and it was heart-breaking to leave her, for she was old enough to recognise us and always cried when we left. But when the isolation period was up, she came home and we heaved a sigh of relief to have our beautiful little girl back safely.

It was the time when the Post Office were changing all the old manual exchanges to automatics, and some overtime did become available. I had been promoted to 'jointer's mate' being mate to a man who had been employed by the Post Office since leaving school and earning quite good pay. There were three gangs working in Bolton, all on the same project, and, whilst two of these were given overtime, needless to say I was in the gang that wasn't. One of the lads told me that this was because my immediate boss had somehow fallen foul of *his* superior, and that consequently, his gang got no overtime. As we were all engaged on the same job, I thought this unfair and went to see one of the engineers to ask for my share of overtime. He was the one who had the needle for my boss, and he turned me down flat.

'You were told when you started that we did not guarantee overtime.' he said.

I agreed that this was so, but added that I wasn't looking for any guarantee, merely the same treatment as the others.

But he was adamant. 'No.'

By this time, the superannuation money had gone, and things were tight, so I then asked to be transferred to maintenance, who were responsible for sorting out faults. They did get overtime, although they were liable to be called out in emergencies at any time of night, but again he flatly refused. I was getting a bit hot under the collar by this time, so I said that I may as well leave, and he told me that was my prerogative. I went back to the jointers' room, wrote out my resignation and handed it to my boss, who accepted it reluctantly, then went back to work.

The following day, I had a visit from another engineer, a very decent man, who asked if it was true I was leaving. I told him it was, and when he asked why, I explained.

'Is that the only reason?' he asked.

I told him it was.

'If you get some overtime, will you stay?'

I said that if I got the same as the others I would, as I liked the job and my work-mates, and certainly didn't *want* to leave.

'Leave it with me,' he said.

An hour or so later he was back.

'What about an hour each day and Saturday morning?' he asked, and when I told him that was fine he said he would go back to the garage and cancel my notice.

When we worked out of Blackburn, we used to start packing up at three thirty, as we finished at four thirty and we had to pack all the stuff into the van before returning to the garage in Shorrock Street. At half past three, the jointer turned off the gas-ring that we used to keep the cables dry, as a prelude to beginning to packing up the gear.

'Hang on Ken,' I said, 'Jimmy says we can have an hour every night.'

He began to fold the felt that covered the cables while we worked. 'I want no overtime,' he said flatly. And of course, if the jointer wouldn't work overtime, then his mate couldn't. So when we returned to Shorrock Street, I saw Jimmy, the decent engineer, and told him I would finish that weekend, and when he asked why, and I told him, he just shook his head, which could have meant anything. On the Friday, I collected my wages and my cards.

On Monday morning, the twenty sixth of April 1966, I walked down to the Sun paper mill just off Preston Old Road, at the foot of Moulden Brow, and was the sister mill to the Star. It was the second paper mill to be built in the Roddlesworth valley, the first being at Withnell Fold and known originally as Engine Bottoms, later known as Wiggins Teape. The Star and The Moon, together with the Eclipse, completed the four in the area. The Eclipse was a textile mill and the Moon never opened, being mysteriously burned down before it went into production. The one remaining wall, with window arches, is still visible in the hollow to the north of Preston Old Road, near the ruins of Feniscowles Old Hall, the former home of a branch of the Feilden family.

Unlike the Star, which was a 'white' mill, using pulp and China clay, the Sun was a 'dirty' mill, its production of strong cardboard boxes made from recycled waste. At that time, it had been taken over by the giant Reed Group, just the latest phase in a very chequered history of private and corporate ownership, with the usual boom and bust periods interspersed with actual closures when times were harder than usual. Built in 1874 it had provided employment for several generations of local workers, and to have three generations employed at the same time was not all that unusual. Some of the older people had managed a complete working life without ever having to draw the dole, although they had known the rough times common to the industrial north of England.

It had been a three-machine mill, but number two, which shared a machine-house with number one, was partly dismantled because the directors of Reed Group had planned to close it completely, that is until the idea of running the four-shift system was broached and accepted. On the old three-shift system, the machines shut down every weekend, and this, together with the start-up on the following Monday, was a very expensive business. But if the machines could be run continuously, with only the odd shut for clothing, cleaning and maintenance, then it could be run profitably. I am going into a lot of detail here, because nearly thirty years later, this homely little mill was taken over by a foreign company, who, regardless of its long history, its satisfied customers, its excellent plant and product, low overheads and consistent profit, closed it, made the workforce redundant and accepted a twenty million pound grant from the government of the day, to develop a similar mill down south; a mill that was making similar paper, but at a loss. But that, as they say, is another story.

Those first months when the machines were starting up after a long shut time, were certainly rough on the workers. Machine breaks were frequent and we were making 'broke' faster than we could recycle it. The reeler-house had three re-reeling machines, ancient even then. And then there were stillages for piling the broke and the laps of paper ripped down from the reels through dampness or out of weight or other faults. The volume of this waste was such that at times we could hardly find the stillages under it and at the end of eight hours straight toil, we may have cleared half of it, only to find on returning for the next shift that we were back where we started. It was back-breaking and heart-breaking, but we persevered, while the turnover in new arrivals and departures was almost comical. I remember one man clocking in at eight on his first morning and by nine was on the bus heading back to Blackburn. He was an exception, but others came, stayed a few days or weeks – some even months – and left. The ones who stayed longer than a few months tended to be the ones who would stay a long time.

After I had been there about a year, I was asked if I would like to go into the size kitchen, and as I didn't really like working in the machine house, I agreed. Whilst working at the Yarn Dyers, I had witnessed a very nasty accident, when the foreman's arm was caught by the drive-shaft of a dyeing machine and horribly mangled. I had been wary of machinery ever since. The size 'kitchen' was an area in what had once been the salle, when a different kind of paper had been produced, and the plant consisted of a slurry tank, where potato starch and water were mixed, a cooking-tank, where the slurry was 'cooked' and enzymes added. The cooked size was kept in storage tanks on the floor below, until it was fed to the size-press on the machines. When I started, number three machine did not have a size-press, so the job was really quite comfortable and I was my own boss, working alone. So long as there was always size, no-one bothered me.

I enjoyed working in the size kitchen, although it was very dusty, the fine starch getting everywhere. I used to keep some old clothes at work and change into them when I arrived. My boss was the mill chemist, and although the office remained constant, the incumbents changed several times over the near-thirty years I remained.

Although the actual filling of the slurry tank with starch was carried out by hand, the cooking and everything else was done by electronics, and Alan Lawson, the man in charge of the electronic section became a very good friend. Ironically, as a young man just demobbed from the army, he had contracted polio, and the disease left him with a limp and limited use of his left arm. He had only been home three weeks when the disease struck and as the polio virus had an incubation period of three *months*, he must have contracted the virus while serving, and therefore had a claim to an army pension. But, as usual, the army ducked their obligations.

He had a couple of apprentices and between them, they did some very extensive and high quality installation work and his section seldom gave any trouble. He and his men were conscientious and reliable and the directors never knew or appreciated the enormous contribution they made to the success of the mill.

We also had a first-rate engineer in Dennis Webb, a man from Kent, who had risen from apprentice and who was not only a good theory man but also extremely competent in the practical side. He was not above taking off his jacket and 'mucking in' with his workforce when necessary. Alan, Dennis and the maintenance staff did an excellent job with the old machinery and when the machines finally settled down, we had a great little mill with a good product and a homely atmosphere. It was, as some of us appreciated, like a rather rough but happy family.

As a child I had been regarded as 'precocious' for my quick responses to certain remarks and/or situations. 'Cheeky' would be nearer the truth, and in some cases my tongue would respond more rapidly than my brain which often caused embarrassment or anger. Like the time I was washing my hands in preparation to clocking off, and in the washroom mirror, glimpsed the approach of a workmate to the adjacent basin. He was wearing his crash-helmet, a white dome affair, and immediately I gave a mock start and said 'My God, I thought you'd gone bald.'

The man, an ex-pat Londoner, was not noted for his sense of humour but was noted for his almost complete baldness. The look he gave me, as I scrubbed my hands to the bone in acute embarrassment, would have withered stronger men than me, but there was more to come.

Hurrying from the mill, I found myself in step with another colleague who, as he was passing my street, offered me a lift in his car, and as we approached the car park, I told him of my gaffe. And it was only when I noticed his blank stare that I realised that he too sported a centre parting that reached down to his ears! It was a long, cold wait for the bus.

Sometimes it wasn't really my fault. One day I had collected my pay and had promised to get Mavis some cigarettes on my way home. It was possible to buy fags from the Time Office at the paper mill but they didn't stock her brand, so I called at a pub nearby. I was standing in the crush, waiting for a chance to catch the barman's eye, when two ex-workmates from the GPO Telephones walked in.

'Well, look who's here,' exclaimed Charlie, offering his hand.

Now Charlie was one of those people who can immediately catch a barman's eye, and after ordering his drink he asked me what I would have.

'Nothing, thanks,' I said, adding truthfully, 'I don't drink.'

His smile became a little fixed.

'Don't drink? Well what are you doing in a pub?' he asked, reasonably enough.

'Oh, I just popped in for some fags.'

Immediately, he took out his packet.

'Have one of these, while you're waiting,' he said. A very open-handed man was Charlie.

'No thanks,' I said, 'I don't smoke.'

His smile was no longer fixed, which was proved by the fact that it had completely disappeared. I didn't need to bother trying to explain, as he, with a rather obvious nudge to the ribs of his pal, suddenly noticed a friend in the corner, and with a muttered apology, drifted off. Ah well, what's the use, I thought.

For close on twenty years, my dad had worked at Messrs. Park Brothers, who made batteries for both industry and the armed forces. His job was a hard one; there was a large tank where the pigs of lead were melted, and he had to keep this topped up by carrying the pigs, which weighed half a hundredweight each, up a vertical ladder, to feed into the tank. He worked twelve-hour shifts, days and nights, and as he grew older, he asked for some form of mechanical assistance in raising these pigs, but he was always put off. When he reached the age of sixty-five, he retired, even though the management had the nerve to ask him to stay on, saying that the younger men would not – or *could not* – do the job. He declined to carry on and took his hard-earned retirement, but only a couple of years later, he suffered a heart attack, and although he made a partial recovery, he was never the same man and he died in May of 1970, a few months short of his seventieth birthday. Our one consolation was that he saw his last grandchild, Patricia, born on the eighteenth of March. He was quite weak by then, but Mavis walked the three miles from our house, with Patricia in the pram and placed her in his arms. Ten months later, my mother collapsed and died in the street. A very black year indeed.

I loved him dearly. As a young man he had had seven years of the dole, followed by six years of war, had been nearly killed while saving the life of another man and had had to work hard until the day he retired; but he was always honest and generous. When things had been at their worst, during the Depression, he and my mother had often gone hungry to let us kids have what food there was, and neither of them ever complained about their lot. They were the very salt of the earth, and when he died, he left a gap in my life that nothing could fill. He left no money but no man ever left a greater legacy of unselfish example. I wanted him to live forever, and in my heart and memory, he will.

It was approaching Christmas. In those days the Christmas break was nothing like it later became. We worked on Christmas Eve, sometimes until six p.m. or later. We had Christmas Day and Boxing day off and that was it. New year's day was not recognised as a holiday in the paper industry and it was only when the union got a stronger grip that they got it changed. Eventually, the Christmas shut period became a minimum of ten consecutive days. On occasion, a shift's rest days fell immediately before and again immediately after, so that shift would have nearly three weeks, the break terminating on the morning of the second of January – 'start-up day'. While the mill was shut, much maintenance and alteration work went on during the day, but this terminated at tea time, and I was asked if I would like to carry out fire-watching duties over the shut, along with just one other 'volunteer'.

Well, I made it a rule never to refuse overtime, and, although the rate of pay was very poor, being less than the minimum hourly rate for general duties, I said I would do it. The shifts would be of twelve hours and, with only two of us, one had to do all the twelve-hour days and the other the nights, and as the other man had been asked first, he got the days.

During those nights, the empty mill was an eerie place, with all kinds of odd thuds, sighs, bangs and creaks, and as the only lighting was from the orange emergency lights high in the machine-house roof, we carried a torch, to check in the dark corners, of which there were very many. There were eighteen check points and at each we inserted a key into a leather-cased clock, and with a turn, a record was made on paper tape of the point number and the time clocked. This was later checked by the Safety Officer. We patrolled every hour, the tour taking about forty-five minutes, which left a quarter of an hour between walks. The nights were long and the walking and climbing caused aching legs and blistered heels, especially as there were lots of stairs to climb. After I had completed the last shift, I was glad that my rest days happened to fall on the start-up day.

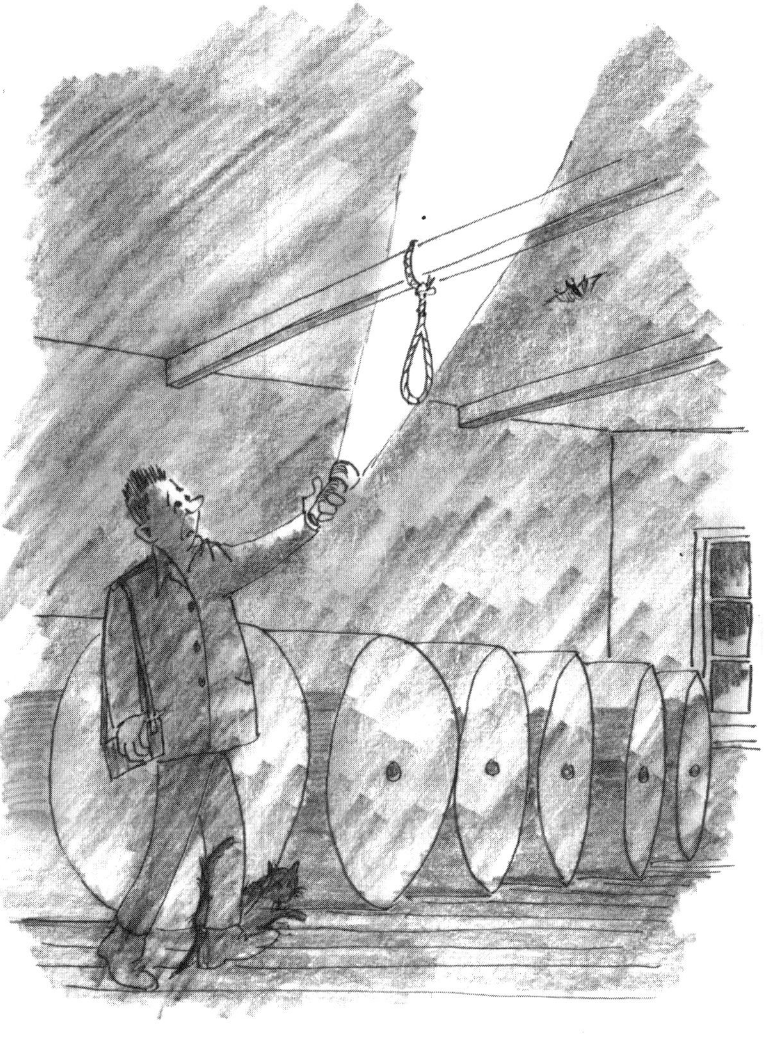

The two of us shared these fire-watching duties for a couple of years, covering the three shuts; Easter, the summer holiday and Christmas, but eventually the union got the rate of pay nearly doubled. Unfortunately, this attracted the greedier ones, so that the fire-watchers now worked only an eight-hour shift, and there was a 'subs' bench, so to speak, because of the number of volunteers. Needless to say, the quality of the cover immediately deteriorated, because the newcomers were interested only in the money, and would find all ways of cutting corners, such as removing the key from the upper points on their first tour and carrying it in their pocket, turning it in sequence, but without having to climb – or check. One man, not knowing that the keys were numbered, used the same key for all the eighteen ' checks', while never even leaving the comfort of the cabin that had been set aside for him. It is only fair to say that not *all* of the men were like this, but the ones who did the job properly could be counted on the fingers of one hand. Complaints had no effect anyway, and I was just relieved that we never had a major fire.

CHAPTER TWENTY THREE

The Turbulent Seventies

After the phenomenally successful rebuild of number three machine, Mr Webb had become manager of the Sun paper mill. As I said earlier, the old number three was slow and did not have a size-press, which restricted its output to 'Chipboard' and 'Blueline' – neither product as profitable as the sized 'Reedchem', from which strong packing boxes were made.

Under Mr Webb's overall charge, being, at that time, the Mill Engineer, the rebuild, using mainly reclaimed parts from the old number two machine, was completed a full five days before schedule. After the start-up – always a tricky period in the paper industry – the machine was making paper within *thirty minutes*, an unprecedented performance. This feat of engineering was justly rewarded when the then manager, Mr Massam, was promoted and left for the south of England, and Mr Webb took over.

I had been a First-Aider since 1967 and had to attend refresher course every three years, a five-day stint at the Medical Centre at Darwen. Although there was much to remember, I always enjoyed the course, and particularly the daily dinner in the canteen of the parent company, Crown Paints. It was a luxury to have a full hour for dinner and to have a free meal.

There were some humorous little interludes on these courses and one in particular springs to mind, when the laugh was on me. There were about ten of us that first morning, under the instruction of George Dunbar, a full-time St John's Ambulanceman. After about fifteen minutes, the door of the room was thrown open and in staggered an elderly man wearing the white coat of a lab worker. His eyes were wide and his right hand was clutched around his left wrist, on which was an enormous blister, surrounded by a large area of inflamed skin.

'Lab ...,' he gasped, as we all swivelled to take in this spectre, 'explosion....'

Being nearest the door - the lesson of the 'denims' incident at Bridgnorth had obviously been unheeded - and genuinely concerned for the poor sod, I leapt up and guided him towards the chair that George had luckily (!) set in place by the sink, and the table that held dressings, lotions and other paraphernalia connected to the course. I suddenly thought, as he took the seat, that everyone else – and George in particular – seemed to be taking this tragic intrusion rather lightly.

'What's up?' demanded George of the casualty, casually lighting a cigarette.

The casualty groaned and displayed his arm. 'Scalded.'

By this time, the penny had dropped and I made to sidle back to my seat, but George had other ideas.

'Well, seeing you are on your feet Frank, you may as well carry on,' he said.

Cursing inwardly and conscious of the critical eyes of the other students, I set about helping the man as if it had been a genuine accident, although I could now see that the 'blister' was in fact, a lump of white petroleum jelly, and the 'inflamed' area merely some dyestuff. Still, they were cunningly contrived. I had already seated him, so I began my ministration. I knew that the treatment for any burn, be it dry or wet, was cold water, so I took the jug that was on the table and turned to the sink.

'Don't put any water in, just mime,' said George, 'and keep up a running commentary as you go, telling us what you're doing and why.'

'I am going to fill ……' I had reached only this far in my running commentary when I heard a groan, followed by a slithering noise and a thud, and when I turned round, the casualty was lying on the floor. What the hell do I do now? I thought, as I put down the jug and knelt over the man to whom I was beginning to take a strong dislike. I couldn't lift him unaided, and no-one else was jumping to help, so I turned him into the recovery position, careful to keep his 'injured' arm uppermost. At this juncture, George took on the role of the ubiquitous 'helpful bystander,' while at the same time offering genuine suggestions.

'Want a lift to get him on the chair?'

I would have to sort out which were the genuine bits as I went along, and I decided this was OK. Between us, George and I helped him up and sat him on the chair, where the casualty lolled, head back and eyes closed, moaning softly. I was beginning to hate his rather handsome face.

'Lean his uninjured side against the wall,' said George, 'so that he can't fall.'

Meanwhile the casualty had regained consciousness and was nodding assent.

'What about taking his watch off?' said George helpfully.

'Of course,' I thought. 'I should have thought of that.' I wasn't shaping up very well.

'Mind you don't catch the blister,' said George, as I carefully slid my fingers under the expanding strap.

I expanded it as wide as it would go and carefully slid it off, well clear of the blister, while George, at my elbow, craned his neck to see every move, puffing smoke into my face and dropping ash onto the table and its contents. I wasn't sure whether he was in his bystander role or not, so I decided to tolerate things for a while. I laid the watch on the table and now that the wound was clear of obstruction, picked up the jug again. 'I have removed the watch, and I am going to pour ....'

'What are these?'

There was no doubt that George was now the 'helpful' bystander, for he was rooting through the contents of the glass-fronted cupboard.

'Leave that,' I said sternly, just as a snore sounded from the casualty, who, unable to fall to the floor, had decided to merely faint. The bastard.

I set down the jug and turned to the casualty, my face getting quite red with embarrassment at the titters from the safe students gathered like vultures over a twitching body.

'Shall I phone for an ambulance?' asked the helpful bystander.

'Ah,' I thought, 'why not?' Best suggestion the bloody nuisance has made. Get him off my back. And immediately the thought impinged. 'Do I *need* an ambulance?' I'm supposed to be a responsible, calm and competent First Aider. Can't I deal with this? What would I look like if I sent for an ambulance and the casualty suddenly recovered and all he needed was a cold compress?

'No, don't call anyone,' I said, feeling smug at my sharpness, 'but go and see if you can find his foreman and tell him I want to see him. Quickly.'

Off went the helpful bystander, taking his fag-ash with him. The casualty blinked, groaned, swallowed and sat up straight, staring round dazedly. I took up the jug, fighting a strong temptation to shatter it over his grey head.

'I am going to fill the jug with cold water and ….'

'Where's me watch?'

I stopped and gaped at the swine. How could I ever get any further if he ……*Watch*? I turned to the table where I had put it among the paraphernalia. Still there − the paraphernalia. The watch? No. Looked like an expensive one, too. More titters from the audience of sadists. The watch had been there *up to the time the helpful bystander had gone.* Now, my head was spinning between the charade and reality, and I think George took pity on me. He returned, minus the fag, and bearing the watch and a broad smile.

'I think we've had enough fun at poor Frank's expense,' he said, 'but we'll just go through the things he did and the things he *should* have done.'

Well, as he reached each point, (talk to the man, get the history of the incident, check his colour as you sit him safely, calm him, reassure him, and so on) everything seemed to be so very *obvious*, like Sherlock Holmes explaining how he solved the mystery by *observing* all the clues that had been as readily available to *us*, who had merely *seen* them. Well, that was how things went on the courses; sound instruction, a little laughter, a little make-believe, and then the exams, oral and practical. But I made sure I *never* sat nearest the door on future refreshers.

I can't leave the First Aid business without telling you about Eric. For some jobs we had to pair off and I was teamed with this large, jovial young man who was very popular for his unfailing good humour. That he was good-humoured is undeniable. But also undeniable is the fact that he was a queer shape. Well, not that exactly, but ... sort of .... how can I describe him? The nearest thing I can think of is a dolphin. You know, sort of pointed at both ends and round and sleek in the middle. Come to think of it, his facial features were quite similar, with heavy-lidded eyes and a wide mouth that turned up at the corners. Anyway, we pairs were to practice applying dressings and arm-slings to each other, and while he had no difficulty bandaging me, it was rather different when we swapped roles.

Eric had no shoulders. From his ears, he sloped gracefully downwards and outwards to a large waistline before returning to a pair of flipper-like 'ten to two' feet. There was no point where I could anchor a sling. Every time I tried, the damned thing slipped inexorably down where his shoulder should have been, and tightening it only tended to force his fist up his nostrils. And the more I tried, the more frustrated I became and the more his dolphin smile widened. In the end, George, the instructor, agreed to take it as done.

Even less easy was turning Eric over into the recovery position. At the beginning of the course, a very slight young girl had been brought in to show how easy it was when done properly. She was great. With a body-weight of about six stone, she whipped a twelve-stone volunteer over as easily as turning back a bed-sheet. It was all down to the pre-positioning of the arms and legs, and it looked very easy indeed. And so it turned out - for everyone else. But I had Eric.

I lay on my back, feigning unconsciousness, as we had been instructed. We were not to assist in any way by using our own muscles. Eric crossed an arm over my chest, a leg was bent at the knee, his hands gripped my shirt and, without the least assistance on my part, I was rolled easily over onto my face. My face was half-turned so as not to impair breathing, my limbs arranged so that I was both comfortable and safe. Now we swapped places.

Eric lay on his back, looking like a cross between a contented baby and a stranded whale, and I knelt beside him and pulled an arm over, laying the other straight by his side. So far, so good. I even got his leg crossed over without too much trouble, although he was so relaxed and heavy I think it was possible he had fallen deeply asleep. Now to roll him over. But I found that, to compound the absence of shoulder and the protuberance of his belly, he also wore a nylon shirt!

Now how the hell do you manage to get a firm grip on something as smooth as silk and as slippery as lubricating-oil? The more I tugged, the faster I lost my grip on the nylon, and after a while, when everybody else had completed this relatively simple exercise, and had taken seats to watch my efforts, I was sweating profusely and greatly tempted to stand up and kick six bells out of the grinning Eric. But somehow, I accomplished it, and vowed to add dolphin-like humans to my list of things to avoid.

A lot of money was being spent on the mill. Number three machine was speeded up by adding more drying cylinders, and it now overtook number one as the prime profit-maker. A new screening plant was installed, making a better sheet, and a brand-new loading bay was built to accommodate the longer trailers. We were doing well, the order book was full, the customers were satisfied and the proposed Channel Tunnel was far off, in terms of both distance and time. But, of course, nothing stands still.

Joan Waring and Elsie Dinham were the ladies who cleaned the office block every evening, working between five and nine. Apart from being excellent cleaners, they were both of impeccable character and one evening, they reported a very strange occurrence. One of the maintenance staff had come to the time office to collect a key, and as he was signing the sheet, Joan came through the door that separated the time office from the reception area.

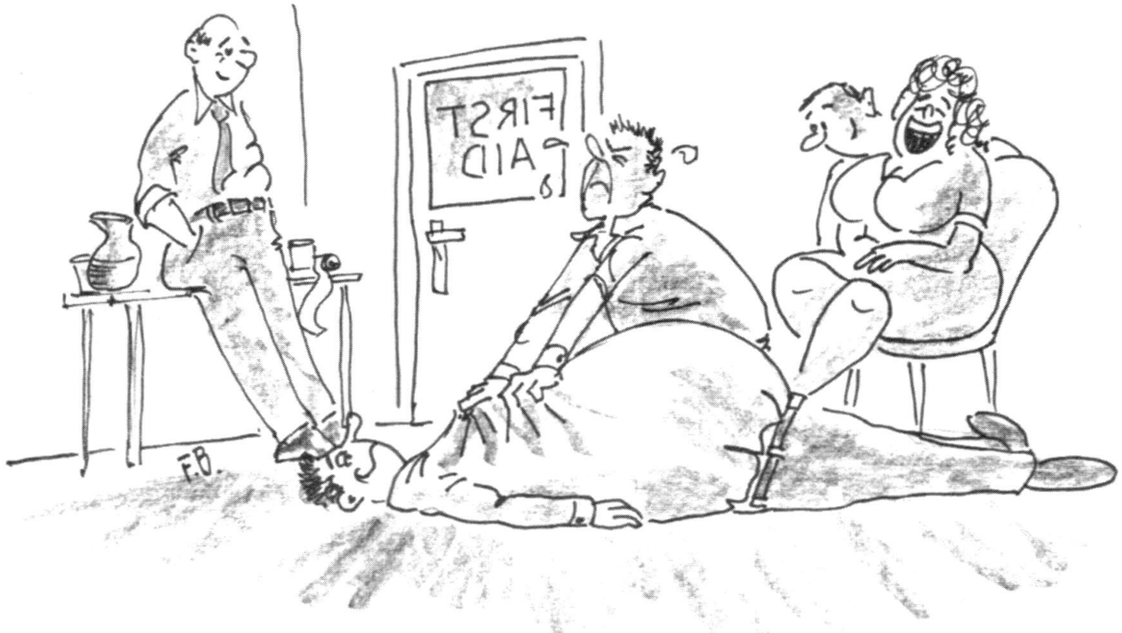
FIRST AID

She looked a little apprehensive and she asked me if anyone had gone through the reception area and upstairs. All of the offices were in that block and could only be reached via the reception area. The time was about half past eight, and the offices had been unoccupied since five o'clock.

There were just three ways into the reception area; by the main doors, by a door at the end of a corridor that connected with the laboratory and test lab, and through the door where Joan now stood, connecting the time-office with reception. The main door had been locked as usual by Joan herself when she collected the office keys at five and no-one had passed the time office, which left only the door at the end of the corridor.

'It must have been somebody coming up from the mill,' I said.

She shook her head. 'We were both in the kitchen (whose only door led off the corridor in question) and if anybody had come that way, we would not only have heard them, but would have seen them, too.'

I could only repeat that no-one had passed the time office, a fact verified by Jimmy Stuart, the electrician who had collected the key.

Joan was adamant. Somebody walked across the reception area. The floor was tiled, and the footsteps sounded quite loud. They went upstairs and a door on the first landing opened and closed.'
By this time, Elsie had arrived from the kitchen, no doubt nervous at being alone, and as both women were upset, I asked Jimmy if he would stay by the time office while I investigated. He readily agreed. If there *was* anyone there, I wanted someone around when I flushed him out. I took the master key, which would open every door in the office block, and went upstairs.

I checked every room, including the toilets, being careful to lock each one behind me once I'd searched it. There were three floors, the top one housing the motor that operated the lift, a huge water cistern, and all the cleaners' stores of mops and dusters, etc. I even checked the French doors that opened onto the roof of the kitchen, into which was set a glass skylight. At the end of the tour, I had checked every room, every cupboard, every inch of floor-space, and had locked all the doors behind me, so that if anyone *was* hiding, he was now a prisoner. Finally, I checked the lift itself and returned to the two women and Jimmy, who confirmed that no-one had come down.

After the careful check, the two women were feeling a little easier, but still not fully reassured.

'We both heard them.' said Joan, and Elsie was quick to confirm this.

'Somebody walked right across the reception floor, went upstairs and then we heard a door open and close. And it wasn't anybody coming through from the mill, because as I said before, they would have had to pass the kitchen, and we would have *seen* as well as heard them.'

'Well.' I said, 'there's certainly nobody upstairs, and I've locked all the doors, but if you have to go up for anything, I'll go with you.'

They had one or two things to do, and Jimmy had gone back to his duties. So I locked the time office and went with them, going from office to office until they had completed their work. No sight or sound of anyone, and with their work now finished, and the time near nine, they handed in the keys and waited until it was time to clock out.

'I wonder if it was Cliff?' said Joan, with a nervous little laugh.

Cliff Hocking had died just a day earlier, and it had been a long-time habit for him to come down every evening around the time when the shift foremen were changing over, to have a word in the foremen's' cabin in number one machine house. But he very often visited his own office first. *And his office was on the first floor.* As a matter of fact, I had been thinking along the same lines, but had said nothing because I didn't want to put ideas of ghosts and haunting into their heads. The incident remained a mystery, and now the mill, the offices and the house where Cliff had lived at the time, have all been demolished, so I suppose it will remain a mystery.

In the late eighties, Reed Group decided to sell the three paper-making units, two of which were near neighbours, 'The Lower Darwen Mill' and 'The Sun,' the third down south. There were rumours of both American and Japanese interest, but the gossip was that Reed preferred that the mills remain in British hands and eventually, the senior staff raised enough money for a management buy-out. There was obviously much that we didn't know about going on backstage, and before long we had changed hands again. The management investors made some very hefty profits for their short-term ownership.

One afternoon, whilst relieving Bob Greenhalgh, he asked how I liked the new bosses.

'What new bosses?' I asked, and he told me that the three mills had been bought by a Swedish company, known as SCA.

I was never much concerned about things I didn't understand, so merely shrugged. But before long, something of grave importance happened. The employees at 'The Lower Darwen Mill' were given ninety days notice that the mill was going to shut. This was a bombshell, especially to the staff. A few of them were found jobs at Sun, and there was a scheme to make up an extra shift there, reducing the normal working week and altering the arrangement to accommodate the extra shift, but this came to nothing.

This caused much concern and speculation for us at the Sun, for to our new bosses, with no interest in our local traditions and records, we were merely a six-monthly balance sheet. In the early days of 1992, Geoff Mayoh, who had succeeded Cliff Hocking as the Sun production manager, attended a meeting at Lower Darwen, having been called by our new bosses to set our minds at rest. When he returned he told me our jobs were safe for the next five years at least. If this was true, then it was a big relief, but there were many who were sceptical, and I was one of them.

In the spring, the mill painter Jimmy McGillick, was ordered to finish painting the mill frontage. He had painted about three quarters of it a couple of years earlier, but had been taken off before he had completed it. While Jimmy was thus engaged, a former Reed Transport driver came chatting through the time-office window.

'That's how it started at Lower Darwen.' he said, nodding his head towards the scaffolding at the bottom of the mill.

I didn't know what he was talking about, so I asked him to elucidate.

'That's what they did before they shut it,' he said. 'Painted the bloody mill all through then shut it. It'll happen here.'

He was serious, too, but I recalled the meeting that Geoff had attended. Our jobs were all right. Or were they? I felt distinctly uneasy, and so did certain others, one of whom had predicted on more than one occasion that we would be shut 'By Christmas.'

One afternoon, I had been out in the car and called at a local chip-shop. As I got out of the car, I met Bill Weall, a reelerman.

'Heard the news?' he asked.

'About what?'

'We're shutting,' he said. It was the ninth of June 1992, mere months since the meeting called to 'set our minds at ease' and assure us that our jobs were safe for 'five years at least.'

Of course there was uproar among the workers. We were a damned good mill, making a constant profit. We had spent millions of pounds on new plant over the last few years, we had a good product; satisfied customers, a good workforce and small office staff, which kept overheads down. And we had a history of paper-making that went back well over a century. Our new owners were adamant. There would be ninety days notice, the mill would close its doors for the last time on September the thirteenth. Despite all our protests, they would not budge. We were offered what the SCA described as generous redundancy pay, one and a half week's pay for every year of service, and told that this offer would be re-thought if we continued to argue. And while they were threatening to cut our redundancy pay, the government was preparing for them a nice little 'grant' of twenty million pounds. I was then, and still am, firmly convinced that the Sun paper mill was shut and nearly two hundred people thrown onto the scrap-heap with the full connivance of the government. Our mill – and indeed the workforce – was nothing special to them, we were just some of the untold thousands whose living had been taken from them by the people who play monopoly with our lives.

I worked my last shift on the ninth of September. My rest days fell on the tenth and eleventh and I was told I needn't report for work after my rest days. The bosses said the redundancy pay was generous, but in reality, they had robbed me of three years earnings, for at the age of sixty two, who would be interested in me?

In the winding-down period, a small 'shop' was set up, staffed by people who tried to help some of the workers find other jobs, and in a few cases they were successful. I was offered a temporary job as a security officer – at £1.50 per hour! I declined.

So what did the future hold for me? I didn't know. But I did have hopes and ambitions. I would draw cartoons, I would write stories, I would keep busy, maintain interest. In 1996, Punch magazine, which had been 'dead' for a long time, re-floated, and they bought some of my cartoons. Thus encouraged, I submitted to other publications, and had some success. I also sold a few articles and together with my younger son Christopher, published a local history book which sold quite well. At present, I am finishing my second detective story. As I said at the beginning of this ramble down Memory Lane, I am a graduate of the University Of Life, and I thoroughly recommend the course.